The Guardian of
Every Other Right

BICENTENNIAL ESSAYS ON THE BILL OF RIGHTS

Co-sponsored by Oxford University Press
and the Organization of American Historians

Kermit L. Hall, General Editor

EDITORIAL BOARD

Michal Belknap, Harold M. Hyman, R. Kent Newmyer,
William M. Wiecek

FAIR TRIAL
Rights of the Accused in American History
David J. Bodenhamer

THE GUARDIAN OF EVERY OTHER RIGHT
A Constitutional History of Property Rights
James W. Ely, Jr.

THE SHAPING OF THE FIRST AMENDMENT
1791 to the Present
Paul L. Murphy

PROMISES TO KEEP
*African Americans and the Constitutional Order,
1776 to the Present*
Donald G. Nieman

OTHER VOLUMES ARE IN PREPARATION

Preface

A widely shared desire to acquire and enjoy property has long been one of the most distinctive features of American society. Defense of economic rights figured prominently during the American Revolution and at the Constitutional Convention of 1787. The founding generation stressed the significance of property ownership as a safeguard for political liberty against arbitrary government as well as the economic utility of private property. Mirroring this attitude, the Supreme Court throughout much of American history has championed property rights against legislative interference. This exercise of judicial authority has produced more than its share of dramatic moments, perhaps the most notable being the Court's defense of economic liberty in the 1930s, which threatened the New Deal and precipitated a constitutional crisis.

Despite an impressive literature dealing with constitutional history, there is no work which provides an overview of economic rights and the Constitution. This book seeks to trace the pivotal role of property rights in fashioning the American constitutional order. It emphasizes the interplay of law, ideology, politics, and economic change in shaping constitutional thought. A work of synthesis, this volume moves rapidly over many issues that deserve more complete treatment. Yet I hope that this concise survey will encourage a better understanding of the central place of property rights in American constitutional history, and provide a historical perspective on the contemporary debate about economic liberty.

Numerous individuals made significant contributions toward the completion of this book. I owe a special debt to Kermit L. Hall, the general editor of the OAH Bicentennial Essays. He provided constant encouragement and sage advice. Michal R. Belknap and Harold M. Hyman, members of the editorial board, offered helpful suggestions on the manuscript, as did R. Kent Newmyer for chapters 1, 2, and 3. David J. Bodenhamer and Jon W. Bruce read the entire manuscript and deserve particular thanks for their insightful comments. David Partlett and Nicholas Zeppos read large parts of the work, giving both encouragement and valuable counsel. I also benefited from the specialized knowledge of Jason S. Johnston and Robert K. Rasmussen. Institutional support was also important. I am deeply grateful to Howard A. Hood and Peter Garland of the Vanderbilt University law library for their skill and patience in locating materials. Dean John J. Costonis provided financial assistance, and kindly granted me released time to complete the manuscript. I wish to thank Martha Waggoner for her highly effective secretarial services.

The editorial staff at Oxford University Press was consistently supportive and helpful. Nancy Lane and David Roll handled this project with skill and diligence. The manuscript was copyedited with care by Margaret Yamashita.

My daughter, Elizabeth Ely Brading, read the manuscript and made suggestions which enhanced the volume's style and clarity. This book is dedicated to my wife, Mickey, in a deep appreciation for many years of love, friendship, and support.

Nashville, Tenn.   J.W.E., Jr.
March 1991

Contents

The Guardian of
Every Other Right

Introduction

For decades the protection afforded to property and economic rights under the Constitution has been of scant concern to judges and scholars. The topic, however, never entirely disappeared from view. In 1955 Justice Felix Frankfurter observed: "Yesterday the active area in this field was concerned with 'property.' Today it is 'civil liberties.' Tomorrow it may be 'property' again."[1] As Frankfurter predicted, in recent years there has been a revival of interest in property issues among courts and commentators. Accordingly, it seems a propitious moment to reassess the role that property and economic rights have played in American constitutional history.

Throughout much of American history, economic liberty was an essential component of constitutionalism. From the time of Chief Justice John Marshall, the Supreme Court has favored the creation of a national market and safeguarded the rights of property owners. Moreover, property rights have often been associated with transcendent political values. In 1897, for example, Justice John M. Harlan declared: "Due protection of the rights of property has been regarded as a vital principle of republican institutions."[2] The protection given to property was fully consistent with one major theme of American constitutionalism—the restraint of government power over individuals. Historically, property ownership was viewed as establishing the economic basis for freedom from governmental coercion and the enjoyment of liberty. Accordingly, a study of the constitutional status of property and economic interests reveals much about the attitudes and aspirations of successive generations.

3

Any investigation of the rights of property under the Constitution poses a series of difficult threshold questions. Why do we recognize rights in private property? Does private ownership promote some societal advantage? What are the parameters of ownership? Can one own a human being or an intangible concept such as an invention? What rights does ownership entail? Did thinking about private property change as American society moved from an agricultural to an industrial society? How did the growth of business corporations influence attitudes toward property ownership? These questions raise important concerns associated with the study of property rights.

The overriding issue, however, is the extent of constitutional protection for property and economic rights. The framers of the Constitution were vitally concerned with the need to safeguard property rights. Dissatisfaction with the handling of economic issues by the state governments was a major factor behind the drive for the Constitution. Yet for all of their devotion to property, is is apparent from the text of the original Constitution that the framers were initially content to rely on institutional arrangements to secure the rights of property owners. The bicameral legislative body, an independent judiciary, and the other checks and balances established by the Constitution were expected to create a political climate in which property interests would be safe. Indeed, the framers entrusted Congress with broad power to regulate interstate and foreign commerce. Only the contract clause—"No State shall . . . pass any . . . Law impairing the Obligation of Contracts"—provided a specific guarantee for existing economic relationships, and that clause did not restrict Congress.

This almost exclusive reliance on political institutions was altered by the ratification of the Bill of Rights in 1791. The Fifth Amendment contained two important clauses dealing with property: "No person shall be deprived of life, liberty or property without due process of law; nor shall private property be taken for public use, without just compensation." Like other portions of the Bill of Rights, these clauses were designed to limit the scope of majority rule over matters deemed fundamental in a free society.

Notwithstanding these important constitutional safeguards, owners in this country have never enjoyed absolute dominion over their property. For example, under the common law doctrine of nuisance, owners could not use their land in a manner that unreasonably interfered with their neighbors' property. Moreover, community customs permitted hunting on unenclosed land and access to bodies of water. The regulation of certain businesses, such as taverns and ferries, was also well established in the colonial era. Individuals can be divested of property by taxation. An even more drastic source of interference with property rights is eminent domain, the power to compel a transfer of property from a private owner to the government for a public purpose. The Constitution does not expressly confer eminent domain authority, but the existence of such power has long been viewed as an inherent aspect of sovereignty.

The constitutional protection of property rights has at times been a highly controversial topic. Some maintain that in safeguarding economic liberty, courts foster competition, enhance political independence, and support a system grounded on property and private enterprise. Others picture constitutionalized property as a barrier to reforms and income redistributions designed to assist the disadvantaged and as a threat to the welfare state.

Indeed, the Supreme Court's historic role of supporting economic rights has sometimes generated allegations of class bias, sentiments that have been echoed by contemporary observers. "The federal courts," one scholar charged, "have through most of the country's history been the guardians of wealth and property against the excesses of democracy."[3] Such a sweeping generalization surely requires qualification. There is, of course, some truth in the contention that the Supreme Court has often aided creditors and entrepreneurs against the claims of debtors, employees, and farmers. But at no time has the Court blocked all regulatory or redistributive legislation. Furthermore, judicial review of economic and social legislation, such as health and safety regulations, has not always resulted in rulings favorable to business interests. On a more sophisticated level, one may question whether this complaint is misdirected. The Constitution and the Bill of Rights, after all, contain several express provisions to safeguard economic interests, and the Supreme Court can hardly be expected to render them nugatory. The underlying source of friction is that reformers and liberals favor a more equal distribution of wealth and economic power. Inevitably they place a lower value on property rights than did the framers of the Constitution. Thus, there is bound to be conflict between the egalitarian programs of contemporary liberal jurisprudence and the property clauses of the Constitution.

Another complexity is that disputes over the constitutional protection of economic rights have often been entangled with sectional conflict. Reflecting a rural economy based on the plantation system, the South generated little capital before 1900 and relied heavily on outside investment. The region's debtor position influenced the development of law, as southern lawmakers consistently favored the interests of debtors over those of creditors.[4] Investors, on the other hand, were concentrated in the Northeast, and so inevitably there was a sectional dimension when the federal courts backed the claims of creditors. Assertion of federal court jurisdiction over debt collection litigation and decisions enforcing credit arrangements under the contract clause impacted forcefully on the South, fueling resentment against the Supreme Court. Similarly, the agrarian movement of the late nineteenth century pitted western farmers against eastern capitalists over the regulation of railroads.

It is important to realize that property is a dynamic concept. Forms of wealth change over the course of decades or centuries. In the eighteenth century, land was the principal form of wealth. By the late twentieth century land, though still important, had been eclipsed by intangible personal property such as stocks, bonds, and bank accounts. Many commentators, furthermore, believe that intellectual property, especially patents, will represent the most significant wealth of the next century. Not only does property take different forms, but once-common types of property may cease to have legal recognition. For instance, the abolition of slavery and the Prohibition amendment effectively destroyed property of considerable value.

Likewise, property rights are not monolithic, and there is often conflict among owners with different economic interests. Economic development was a primary objective of Americans in the nineteenth century, but steps to promote growth frequently clashed with the interests of particular property owners. In general, the Supreme Court has looked with favor on the active use of property for commercial ends rather than simply maintaining the status quo. Americans, in J. Willard Hurst's phrase, preferred "property in motion or at risk rather than property secure and at rest."[5] As a consequence, legislators and courts often compelled existing property arrangements to give way to new economic ventures and changed circumstances. New technologies heightened this conflict by rendering obsolete older forms of property and wealth. Thus, in the nineteenth century, railroads gradually superseded canals, and in the twentieth century, air travel captured much of the railroad's business. Nothing in the Constitution inhibited these developments, and indeed judges sought to facilitate improvements despite the loss inflicted on existing types of property.

A study of property and economic rights is also complicated by the distribution of governmental power under the federal system. It was generally contemplated that the states would exercise great latitude in governing their internal affairs. This authority, known as the police power, encompassed the power to enact laws safeguarding the health, safety, and morals of the public. As a result, important areas of economic activity remained largely under state control. Developments at the state level often foreshadowed subsequent federal action. In the early nineteenth century, for instance, state courts and legislators took the lead in formulating eminent domain policy and defining the notion of taking private property rights. A century later state legislatures enacted the first wave of social legislation that regulated working conditions and land use patterns. One cannot understand the constitutional guarantee of property by looking solely at the decisions of the Supreme Court.

The states, however, were especially susceptible to parochial influence and special-interest pressure. Many state laws were designed to suppress competition or to inflict disproportionate costs on out-of-state interests, but such legislation often frustrated national economic policy or threatened private property rights. Reflecting the dictates of economic nationalism, the Supreme Court early established the right to review state laws that burdened interstate commerce. Moreover, the Court initially used the contract clause and later the due process and takings clauses of the Fifth Amendment to fashion a powerful check on state interference with property and business enterprises. Economic rights, then, were among the first to be nationalized by the Supreme Court, thereby setting the stage for numerous constitutional battles that pitted property-minded federal judges against state lawmakers. In contrast, not until the twentieth century did freedom of speech or the rights of criminal defendants find a spot on the docket of federal judges.

Another problem is posed by the separation of powers doctrine and the ongoing debate over the appropriate role for the judiciary in American life. Judicial review of economic legislation raises the question of which branch of government should determine economic policy. Throughout much of our history there has been an undercurrent of judicial suspicion directed toward legislative handling of law affecting property interests. The Supreme Court of Georgia expressed this attitude in 1851, declaring: "The sacredness of private property ought not to be confined to the uncertain virtue of those who govern."[6] Starting from this premise, it was a short step to widespread judicial intervention on behalf of property owners and to increasing supervision of legislative output. Indeed, before the New Deal, judicial review was usually employed to invalidate laws affecting property rights. Critics alleged that such a process was undemocratic and prevented the elected branch of government from responding to novel social problems.

Thinking about property rights is not fixed but has evolved over time in response to changed conditions. By the late nineteenth century, urbanization and industrialization had transformed American society, creating novel pressures directed at traditional concepts of private property ownership. The emergence of the business corporation, coupled with the workings of a free-market economy, exacerbated disparities of wealth, and concentrated tremendous economic power in relatively few hands. Furthermore, land use practices that were acceptable in a largely rural nation appeared in a different light in an urban setting.

Consequently, by 1900 the focus of lawmakers shifted markedly from the promotion of economic growth to its regulation. Legislators sought to redress the unbalanced social and economic situation by, in essence, mandating a redistribution of property in favor of those viewed as disadvantaged. Thus, lawmakers passed statutes to improve working conditions, set minimum wages, regulate the conduct of business, fix prices charged the public, and tax the income of the wealthy. Regulations on land use often fastened significant economic burdens on property owners. Such measures aroused the hostility of conservative judges, resulting in a bitter and prolonged controversy over the constitutional position of property rights. The political and intellectual triumph of the New Deal seemingly settled this conflict by assigning property to a secondary status with only limited constitutional protection, a development that allowed a wide sway for economic regulation.

Finally, any quest for doctrinal precision in the analysis of propery and economic rights is bound to fail. Rules devised for interpreting one clause of the Constitution frequently spill over to another. There has been a large degree of overlap, for example, between legal arguments based on the takings clause and the due process clause of the Fourteenth Amendment.

Further, different constitutional doctrines, such as the concept of economic due process, have bulked large at various periods in America's past. It follows that the history of property rights has not proceeded in a neat and orderly manner. Rather, the story is one of contradiction and ambiguity, in which constitutional policy has been pulled in divergent directions by economic and political forces.

This volume examines the constitutional history of economic and property rights from the settlement of America to the present. It proceeds on the assumption that constitutional law is shaped in a broad political and intellectual context. Thus the book probes the origins of protection for property, examining the English common law tradition, the colonial experience, and the revolutionary struggle. It considers the impact of major political events, including the Jacksonian movement, the Civil War, and the New Deal. Moreover, the work emphasizes the role of ideology in shaping the constitutional status of property.

This book proposes an analytical framework to guide historical investigation; it does not attempt to resolve long-standing disagreements over the breadth of constitutional protection for property. The study suggests three working principles: First, the framers of the Constitution and the Bill of Rights envisioned some degree of federal judicial review of the substance of economic legislation. What criteria should be employed in making this review and which situations justify judicial intervention were and remain topics of intense controversy.

Second, given the framers' concern with protecting property as well as the nearly 150 years of Supreme Court activity in this field, the relegation of property rights to a lesser constitutional status is not historically warranted. The framers did not separate property and personal rights. Significantly, the language of the Fifth Amendment unites safeguards for both liberty and property.

Third, the Constitution seeks to protect several fundamental values, including economic interests, but property is not entitled to preferential treatment. Few constitutional rights are unlimited. Hence, the constitutional protection of private ownership does not imply unrestrained liberty to enjoy the maximum economic advantages of property under all circumstances. The crucial issues are how these competing interests are to be reconciled and which branch of government should strike the balance.

1

The Origins of Property Rights: The Colonial Period

From the very beginning, the settlement of North America was closely linked with economic rights. To Europeans the American continent represented a boundless opportunity for speculation and development; indeed, the prospect of new land was the main economic inducement for colonization. In order to exploit these favorable circumstances, the (British) Crown granted charters conveying vast tracts of land to trading companies and individual proprietors, such as William Penn. Both Virginia and Massachusetts, for instance, were founded by business ventures seeking a profit from colonization. The investors in the Virginia Company of London and the Massachusetts Bay Company were keenly interested in commercial gain. They anticipated revenue derived from annual rents imposed on land grants and from trade with the colonies. Thus, the initial colonies were products of early capitalism in England.

The settlers themselves were also influenced by economic considerations. Without discounting the importance of religious concerns, many colonists hoped to improve their economic position by migration. For instance, John Winthrop, later the governor of Massachusetts, was impelled to leave England by both religious zeal and the hope of financial reward. The availability of land lured settlers to face the hardships of life in the wilderness. As Willi Paul Adams observed, the "acquisition and cultivation of land was the very raison d'etre for the colonies."[1]

English common law provided the legal foundation for property ownership in the colonies. Common law was customary law, deriving its authority from long-established usage. Royal courts in England fashioned the common law into a body of rules that defined and protected property rights. The colonists then selectively adopted English common law as the basis of their jurisprudence. Common law principles, therefore, controlled the use and transfer of land and governed contractual agreements.

The high value attached to landownership by the colonists is best understood in terms of the English experience. In England, as in western Europe generally, land was the principal source of wealth and social status. Yet landownership was tightly concentrated in relatively few hands, and most individuals had no realistic prospect of owning land. Moreover, in theory no person owned land absolutely: All land was held under a tenurial relationship with the Crown. Although there was a bewildering variety of tenure arrangements, property ownership was conditional and involved continuing obligations to a superior. By the seventeenth century, these obligations took the form of *quitrents,* annual payments to the king or overlord. Feudal in origin, the quitrent was regarded as a type of taxation.

Conditions in North America, however, were radically different from those in England, and traditional assumptions about landownership were ill suited to the colonies. Because land was abundant, the trading companies and proprietors attracted settlers by granting land on generous terms: Most colonies outside New England adopted the "headright" system as a means of distributing land. By this device an amount of land was awarded to each person emigrating to the colony. For many years Virginia granted a headright of 50 acres to all settlers. In 1689 the Carolina proprietors promised 150 acres to encourage immigration. Several colonies even offered headright land to indentured servants once their period of service expired. Until the late seventeenth century the headright system was the principal basis of land distribution. Although headrighting was gradually eliminated, individuals could still purchase land for a modest payment. As a further inducement, colonial governments granted land titles in fee simple, the most extensive freehold estate recognized by English common law.

Influenced by religious values and a strong sense of community, the Puritan colonies in New England developed distinct patterns of landownership. To encourage social cohesion, land was granted to groups of settlers through townships and church congregations. The townships then distributed the land as they thought proper. Some New England towns in the early seventeenth century encouraged community life by restricting the transfer of land and by maintaining open fields where villagers worked in common. The New England colonists, however, preferred individual landownership and soon abandoned these early communal arrangements. The Puritans also rejected the notion of dependency implicit in feudal land tenures and in practice adopted outright land-ownership.

Property rights were at the heart of the persistent conflict over New York's singular land tenure system. During the seventeenth century, Dutch settlers introduced patroonships into the Hudson River valley. Similar to English manors, these patroonships were huge tracts of land granted to proprietors. After the English conquest of New York, the Crown confirmed the patroons' titles and made additional grants of large estates. Because the holders of these tracts wished to preserve their domains by leasing rather than selling land, they leased the land to small farmers for long terms in exchange for annual rent and other restrictions. This land tenure system hampered the development of colonial New York and caused considerable social tension. Many farmers resented the land monopoly of a few families and refused to accept tenant status. Unable to obtain land titles in fee simple, settlers preferred to locate in other colonies where such land was available for purchase. There was consistent pressure to break up the great estates, and this smoldering discontent produced serious agrarian riots in 1766. The unrest in New York vividly confirmed the central place of property ownership in colonial thinking. As Cadwallader Colden, the surveyor general, explained, "The hopes of having land of their own & becoming independent of Landlords is what chiefly induces people into America."[2]

The desire of newly arrived colonists to acquire land could not always be contained within legal bounds. Some impatient settlers simply took possession of vacant land without any grant of legal title. Popularly known as squatters, these settlers were often able to secure title based on their occupancy. North Carolina, in particular, attracted an unusually large number of squatters.

Although the English law of land tenure nominally prevailed in much of colonial America, it was largely drained of any substance. Outside New England, landowners were responsible for paying a quitrent to the Crown or a proprietor. But the collection of quitrents was usually lax.

Moreover, the colonists intensely disliked the feudal implications of quitrents, regarding them as a distasteful form of tribute. Consequently, they effectively evaded payment. Periodic attempts to collect quitrents thus produced strife and fanned colonial resentment. Only in Virginia, Maryland, and Pennsylvania were quitrents collected with any degree of success. Quitrents were never recognized in New England, where the colonists stubbornly refused to accept any intimation of a feudal land tenure system and denied English dominion over land titles. In fact, if not in law, the colonists treated their landownership as outright, or allodial, rather than tenurial. In any case, the last vestiges of the quitrent system vanished with the Revolution.

Colonial appreciation of property rights was strongly shaped by the English constitutional tradition. Americans associated property rights with the time-honored guarantees of Magna Carta (1215). Originally forced on a reluctant King John to protect the privileges and property of the nobility, Magna Carta became a celebrated safeguard against arbitrary government. Several important provisions of the Charter protected the rights of property owners. Magna Carta established the principle that consent by a representative body was necessary in order to raise revenue. The colonial insistence on taxation only with consent emanated from the Charter. Further, Magna Carta provided: "No freeman shall be taken, imprisoned, disseised . . . except by the lawful judgment of his peers and by the law of land." With this language Magna Carta secured the rights of owners against deprivation of property without due process of law.

The colonists venerated Magna Carta as part of their birthright as English subjects. As early as 1639 the Maryland assembly declared that inhabitants "shall have all their rights and liberties according to the great Charter of England." Accordingly, colonial laws drew on the principles of Magna Carta to protect liberty and property rights. In words closely resembling those of Magna Carta, the *Laws and Liberties* of Massachusetts (1648) stated that "no mans goods or estate shall be taken away from him . . . unless it be by the vertue or equity of some expresse law of the Country." Both Maryland and Pennsylvania enacted similar provisions protecting owners from the loss of property except by due process. William Penn arranged for the publication of a commentary on Magna Carta in 1687 and urged colonists "not to give away any thing of *Liberty* and *Property* that at present they do . . . enjoy."[3] Colonial judges also were influenced by the charter. In *Giddings v. Brown* (1657) a Massachusetts county court recognized as "a fundamental law" that property cannot be taken "to the use or to be made the right or property or another man, without his owne free consent."

Long before the American Revolution, British imperial policy aroused the colonists to defend their property rights. Following the Stuart Restoration in 1660, English authorities sought to gain stronger control over the colonies. Rejecting the notion that the colonies enjoyed separate constitutional status, officials viewed the colonies as mere possessions of the Crown. One result of this new imperial system was the Dominion of New England, an administrative experiment that consolidated all the New England colonies and New York under a regional government. Created in 1686, the Dominion was ruled by a royal governor, Sir Edmund Andros, and an appointed council. In a sharp break with the constitutional history of the early colonies, there was no representative assembly.

In addition to this loss of self-government, the colonists soon harbored other grievances against the Dominion. When Governor Andros attempted to collect taxes, he faced bitter resistance in parts of Massachusetts. Hoping to force Andros to call an assembly, the colonists protested that according to Magna Carta and English constitutional principles, taxes could not be levied without representation. Although the taxes were eventually collected by force, the Massachusetts colonists had fashioned an important constitutional argument with which to defend their economic rights against the Crown.

Even more ominous was the land policy that Andros adopted. Anxious to undercut the Puritan notion of absolute landownership, imperial authorities asserted that the colonists held land under a tenurial relationship with the king. By attacking the basis of economic independence, the Crown hoped to render the colonies more politically obedient to England and raise revenue from quitrents. Accordingly, Andros required all existing land titles to be reviewed for confirmation and charged a fee for new grants. This move also raised fears that he would impose annual quitrents on landholders. Andros's attack on colonial land titles caused sharp resentment, and many resisted the new land policy. Andros further attempted to curtail speculation in undeveloped land, thereby frustrating the economic activity of land speculators.

The full implications of these troublesome tax and land policies were never realized. In April 1689, after news of the Glorious Revolution reached America, Boston mobs arrested Andros and overthrew the Dominion of New England. This episode underscored the colonists' determination to safeguard, in the words of Suffolk County inhabitants, "our English nations liberties and propertyes" from imperial interference.[4] Further, the colonists' bitter experience with the Dominion made them especially sensitive to arbitrary interference with land titles.

Although blessed with an abundance of land, colonial America faced a chronic labor shortage. Under these circumstances the colonists looked to an unfree labor force. Indentured servants and convicts supplied part of this manpower need. In addition, the colonists, especially in the South, increasingly relied on slave labor by blacks from Africa. English law did not recognize permanent servitude, but the mother country allowed colonial lawmakers to fashion the institution of slavery. At first the law of slavery developed in a piecemeal manner and reflected local custom. However, toward the end of the seventeenth century, as the number of black slaves grew, legislatures enacted comprehensive slave codes that defined the legal status of slaves as a form of property. In 1740 South Carolina declared slaves "to be chattels personal, in the hands of their owners and possessors." Because slaves were property, they could be purchased, sold, inherited, taxed, or seized to pay the master's debts.

Lawmakers, however, drew a distinction between slaves and other types of property. Partially recognizing the human nature of slaves, colonial statutes contained elaborate provisions regulating their treatment. The master was required to feed and clothe his slaves, and he could not kill or overwork them. But as a practical matter, it was often difficult to enforce these restraints. The slave codes also minutely governed the slaves' activities, prohibiting them from assembling, running away, owning goods or livestock, or using firearms. Moreover, it was unlawful to sell liquor to slaves or to teach them to read and write. Finally, crimes committed by slaves received harsher punishment than did equivalent offenses by free persons.

Slavery in the colonial era was not confined to the South. Every colony sanctioned slavery, and New York contained a sizable number of slaves. But slavery was never vital to the economy of the northern colonies. In contrast, there was a tremendous demand for agricultural labor in the South as the plantation system expanded during the late seventeenth century, and so there was a large concentration of slaves there. By the eighteenth century, the ownership of slaves represented an important source of wealth and began to determine social status. Most colonists were little troubled by slavery. Perhaps because their notion of liberty encompassed the protection of property rights, they perceived no inconsistency between the exaltation of liberty and the institution of slavery. By 1750 a largely middle-class society had emerged in colonial America. Most of the colonists owned land, and 80 percent of the population derived their living from agriculture. Likewise, the average city dweller found an abundance of employment opportunities and was better off than his counterparts in England. Even individuals without property shared the acquisitive spirit of the middle class and had a genuine opportunity to achieve better economic circumstances. Cheap land and high wages afforded ample support for Pennsylvania Judge William Allen's assertion: "You may depend upon it that this is one of the best poor Man's Countrys in the World."[5]

In spite of such optimistic accounts, there was a bleak underside to colonial society. For those held in servitude or without marketable skills, life in the colonies was often harsh, even brutal. Economic development in the eighteenth century produced both unequal divisions of wealth and growing class stratification, a situation that generated tension between prosperous urban merchants and less well off farmers. A growing number of indigents also created relief problems for municipal authorities.

Still, colonial society was predominantly property owning and middle class. Economic advancement was within the reach of most colonists, and even day laborers could earn enough to acquire land. These fortunate economic conditions, coupled with the broad distribution of land, explain why the colonists were so receptive to the property-conscious tenets of English constitutional thought. As a group of German settlers in Maryland proclaimed in 1763: "The law of the land is so constituted, that every man is secure in the enjoyment of his property, the meanest person is out of reach of oppression from the most powerful, nor can anything be taken from him without his receiving satisfaction for it."[6]

The colonial attachment to property ownership was powerfully reinforced by intellectual currents in the mother country. For England the seventeenth century was a time of political and religious upheaval, culminating in the Glorious Revolution of 1688. Seeking to justify these events, English political thinkers analyzed the nature of government. The most significant of these Whig theorists was John Locke, who asserted in his famous *Second Treatise on Government* (1689) that legitimate government was based on a compact between the people and their rulers. The people gave allegiance to the government in exchange for protection of their inherent or natural rights. Deviation by the rulers from this fundamental agreement provided grounds for their overthrow.

Of particular importance was the theory of property rights in Locke's political philosophy. According to Locke, private property existed under natural law before the creation of political authority. Indeed, the principal purpose of government was to protect these natural property rights, which Locke fused with liberty. Thus, he asserted that people organized government to preserve "their Lives, Liberties and Estates." Because the ownership of property was a natural right, the powers of government were necessarily limited by its duty to safeguard property. Locke argued that the legislature could not arbitrarily take property and that the levy of taxes without popular consent "invades the *Fundamental Law of Property*, and subverts the end of Government."[7]

It is difficult to overstate the impact of the Lockean concept of property. Strongly influenced by Locke, the eighteenth-century Whig political tradition stressed the rights of property owners as the bulwark of freedom from arbitrary government. Property ownership was identified with the preservation of political liberty. As John Trenchard explained in 1721, "All Men are animated by the Passion of acquiring and defending Property, because Property is the best Support of that Independency, so passionately desired by all Men."[8] Lockean thinking also permeated English common law. In his *Commentaries on the Laws of England* (1765–1769) William Blackstone built on Locke's formulation and defined property rights in sweeping terms. "So great moreover," Blackstone observed, "is the regard of the law for private property, that it will not authorize the least violation of it."[9] Whig political thought profoundly shaped public attitudes in colonial America, and Blackstone's *Commentaries* were widely studied as a summary of English law. Consequently, both their circumstances and philosophical heritage induced the colonists to affirm the sanctity of property rights. To the colonial mind, property and liberty were inseparable, as evidenced by the colonists' willingness to break with England when the mother country seemingly threatened property ownership.

Despite the high standing of property rights, the English Whig tradition did not preclude restrictions on private ownership. Both custom and government regulation limited owners' dominion over their land. For instance, the abundance of game in North America fostered public hunting rights. In sharp contrast with English law, the colonies recognized a general customary right to hunt on privately owned unenclosed land.

Fear of land monopoly caused restrictions on large tracts of dormant land. Many colonists felt that the undue aggregation of undeveloped land by speculators retarded economic growth and frustrated the opportunity for others to acquire property. Hence, the New England colonies frequently required settlement to validate a land grant. Other colonies also attempted to force owners either to sell or to make their land productive. Headright grants commonly specified that the land must be brought under cultivation within a certain number of years. Stating that ''the engrossing and holding of large tracts of land unimproved by several people is very detrimental to the well settling of this Province,'' a 1725 South Carolina act required such landowners either to furnish militia men or to pay a special tax. Similarly, authorities in New York urged reform of the great landed estates and hoped that the vigorous collection of quitrents would compel the landowners to sell undeveloped land.

The use of urban land was also subject to regulation. The growth of colonial cities presented problems of congestion, and so public safety necessitated restrictions on land use. Fire was a constant threat in the cities of colonial America, and much of the burden of fire prevention was placed on individual landowners. Lawmakers thus required that all buildings erected in urban areas be constructed of stone or brick. Defective chimneys required constant public supervision. The storage of inflammable substances, such as gunpowder and straw, was strictly limited. Similarly, city ordinances obligated residents to clean the streets abutting their lots. Municipal authorities also sought to enhance safety on the streets at the expense of residents. New York City, for instance, ordered landowners to hang lights on a pole at night. Further, municipal regulations confined certain obnoxious uses, such as slaughtering cattle, to particular areas.

Likewise, both England and the colonies regulated many aspects of economic life. Mercantilism was the dominant economic philosophy during the seventeenth and eighteenth centuries, and its basic notion was that nations should regulate economic activity to produce prosperity and political strength. Mercantile ideas helped define the relationship between England and its colonies. Under mercantilism the colonies existed largely for the benefit of the mother country. The Navigation Act of 1660, for example, sought to impose a protectionist system on colonial trade. Parliament required that goods imported to the colonies must pass through England. Likewise, most raw materials exported from the colonies could be shipped only to England. Such laws guaranteed English primacy in trading with the colonies but placed a heavy economic burden on the colonists by making them dependent on England. The English mercantile system thus shackled colonial economic aspirations and generated considerable animosity toward the mother country.

Consistent with the mercantilist philosophy, colonial governments regularly intervened in the economy. Lawmakers worked in numerous ways to promote the colonies' economic development. Thus, Virginia legislators encouraged the production of hemp, tar, and saltpeter by providing for the payment of bounties. Several colonies sought to promote the establishment of industry by means of land grants. For example, Maryland offered land to any individuals who would develop ironworks. Other colonies granted land to encourage the production of potash and the construction of mills. In addition, colonial leaders instituted annual commercial fairs in towns and villages as a means to attract trade and hasten commercial growth.

Lawmakers sought to stimulate the development of technology by recognizing the rights of inventors. As early as 1648 the Massachusetts code permitted a monopoly grant for "such new inventions that are profitable for the Countrie." The colonies occasionally awarded special patents to individuals. Declaring "that all due encouragement be given to ingenuity and industry when it tends to the public good," a 1756 South Carolina act vested in one Adam Pedington the exclusive privilege to market "a new method of cleaning rice" for a term of fourteen years. Patents rested on an individual's claim to the fruit of his labor and constituted a reward for inventive activity.

Mercantilist thought also encouraged colonial governments to regulate economic activity for the general welfare of the community. Numerous laws restricted owners in the use and sale of their property. Following the practice in England, certain businesses in the nature of public utilities were closely regulated. Taverns were licensed, a device that both facilitated regulation and limited the number of taverns in an area. Moreover, county courts fixed the rates to be charged for food, drink, and accommodations. Similarly, the colonists treated gristmills as public institutions subject to control. Most colonies regulated the operation of mills and set the toll for grinding grain. The Connecticut code of 1673, for example, provided that a miller "shall be allowed for the grinding of each bushell of Indian corn, a twelfth part, and for other graines, a Sixteenth part."

Throughout the colonial era, legislators were concerned about improving internal transportation. As in England, transportation systems were controlled by colonial officials. Because several of the colonies were divided by rivers, ferry service was particularly important. Lawmakers and county courts therefore made numerous grants of ferriage to individuals. Ferry owners were required to maintain their boats in proper repair and to provide service at all hours. As compensation the ferry operators were authorized to collect a toll set by law. Under English common law such a franchise implied the exclusive right to maintain a ferry within a reasonable distance. Occasionally this limited monopoly to carry passengers was spelled out by statute.

Many colonists distrusted open competition as a mechanism to determine the price of food and goods. In an effort to assure all citizens a fair opportunity to purchase wares, lawmakers established supervised public markets in colonial cities. This municipal regulation of markets sought to eliminate fraud, prevent unfair trading practices, and hold down prices. Weights and measures were standardized. Attempts to undercut the public market were outlawed, and trade in many items was confined to the market. Thus, legislation prohibited forestalling, the custom of buying merchandise on the way to market with the hope of reselling it at a higher price. Market laws also imposed sanitary rules, enforced quality standards, and limited the hours of business.

In another attempt to control market forces, many colonies and localities copied the Assize of Bread from England. Under this statute the weight, quality, and price of bread were regulated by law, and bakers were required to mark their bread to facilitate inspection. The purposes of such legislation were to curb alleged abuses by bakers and to make bread cheap. As explained by the New Hampshire legislature in 1766, it was necessary to establish the assize because "a just proportion between the price of flour and the weight and price of bread, is now a matter of importance, as many people purchase the greater part of their bread of bakers, and without such regulation they were left to judge for themselves.'' Bakers who violated the assize were subject to a fine or a forfeiture of bread. In addition to supervising bread, some localities sought to fix meat prices and to enforce the Assize of Wood regulating the sale of firewood.

Concerned that high interest rates would discourage trade and settlement, colonial legislators commonly enacted usury laws to prohibit the loan of money at an interest rate in excess of a legal ceiling. A 1741 North Carolina measure, for example, declared that ''the settling of Interest at a reasonable Rate, will greatly tend to the Advancement of Trade, and Improvement of Lands,'' and fixed a maximum interest rate of 6 percent. Such legislation restricted the right of the lender to charge whatever interest could be obtained in the open market in order to benefit the community.

Along with establishing prices for services and commodities, lawmakers sporadically attempted to fix wages. Labor was scarce in colonial America, and as a result wages were high. Throughout the seventeenth century, Massachusetts, for instance, experimented with wage regulation. The purpose of such legislation was to stabilize wages for the benefit of employers.

Export restrictions were an important feature of colonial life. Anxious to stabilize prices and protect the reputation of their crops, many colonies established elaborate export controls over staple crops. In 1747 Maryland enacted a comprehensive law that required all tobacco to be inspected at a public warehouse. Unsound tobacco was to be burned. Similar statutes were passed in Virginia and Connecticut. South Carolina compelled exporters of indigo to verify the quality and weight of shipments, and a Pennsylvania statute of 1724 provided for the inspection of flour before export. In order to protect their limited economic resources, the colonies also prohibited the export of essential goods. North Carolina and Connecticut, for instance, prevented the export of hides. Periodic shortages of food caused many of the colonies to place a temporary embargo on grain and other food supplies, thereby protecting local consumers but reducing the farmers' market.

Early manufacturing enterprises also were regulated. Leather was an important product in colonial life because it was used for clothing. Several New England colonies, therefore, enacted laws dealing with the production of leather. These specified the proper techniques for tanning leather and required towns to appoint inspectors to enforce the statutory requirements.

As these examples of governmental promotion and regulation suggest, colonial society often placed the interests of the community above the economic rights of individuals. The colonists could seemingly engage in few business activities without supervision. This impression is misleading, though, and obscures the extent to which the colonists also responded to the emerging doctrine of free trade and entrepreneurial liberty. The demand for regulation should not be exaggerated, and many businesses were unsupervised. There was frequent conflict between private enterprise and public authority. Despite the seemingly pervasive character of colonial regulations, government control of the economy was far from comprehensive.

Several factors limited the impact of colonial business regulations. Lacking a substantial revenue base and adequate supervisory personnel, colonial governments were feeble institutions. Many regulations probably existed only on paper. The colonists circumvented both the Navigation Acts and domestic regulations. Lenders, for instance, easily evaded the usury laws. Licensing and inspection laws were poorly enforced. Travelers in Virginia frequently complained about overcharging by taverns, but the county courts took little action. Resistance to public markets mounted in the mid-eighteenth century, and Boston abandoned the system in 1737. Bakers repeatedly protested the Assize of Bread and forced upward adjustments of prices. A free market for goods and services thus gradually emerged in actuality if not in law. Likewise, wage regulations were undermined by the shortage of labor and the need to attract workers.

Intellectual currents also hastened the decline of economic regulation. Concomitant with regulatory schemes, the colonists voiced concern for greater economic liberty. As early as 1648 *The General Lawes and Libertyes* of Massachusetts provided that "there shall be no Monopolies granted or allowed amongst us." By the mid-eighteenth century, colonists were beginning to stress the potential of economic development. As their focus shifted from scarcity to opportunity, the colonists increasingly viewed commercial regulations as an impediment to growth. Advocates of free trade challenged both the wisdom and the validity of price fixing and controlled markets. Bostonians took the lead in extolling entrepreneurial freedom and criticizing anticompetitive behavior. They attacked the public market "as a breach upon their natural rights and liberties" and argued that market regulations should "not deprive us of the liberty common to Englishmen."[10] Farmers and butchers in New York, unhappy with a rate schedule for meat and other provisions, weaved together political and economic principles to challenge price regulations. In 1763 a group of rural citizens proclaimed: "We thought we were born free Englishmen, and had the liberty, as such, to sell our own effects at our own liberty."[11] In the face of this growing commitment to free enterprise, wage and price regulations appeared to be a relic of the mercantile past.

Such arguments anticipated the landmark *Wealth of Nations* (1776) by the Scottish political economist Adam Smith. A sharp critic of mercantilism, Smith contended that governmental intervention in the economy was unnecessary and likely to prove harmful. According to Smith, the public welfare was best served by allowing each individual to pursue his economic self-interest. He relied on private arrangements rather than government direction to generate wealth and meet the public's needs. As an advocate of entrepreneurial freedom, Smith urged a government with only minimal functions. He argued that the economic law of supply and demand should determine prices and wages. Published the same year as the Declaration of Independence, the *Wealth of Nations* provided the ideological basis for laissez-faire capitalism. The popularity of Smith's ideas in America following the Revolution doomed many of the colonial regulatory practices.

In addition to taxation and regulation, private property was subject to eminent domain, the inherent power of the government to take property for public purposes without the consent of the owner. The authority to take private property was well established in England long before the settlement of North America. This power was, however, gradually qualified by the practice of paying compensation to the owner. The compensation principle was partially recognized by Magna Carta, which declared that the king could not seize provisions without payment. By the seventeenth century, Parliament regularly provided for compensation when property was taken. Blackstone agreed that the legislature could take private property but insisted that the owner was entitled to receive "a full indemnification and equivalent for the injury thereby sustained."[12] He regarded compensation as an established common law principle. Colonial practice with eminent domain was influenced by the English constitutional experience. The colonies did not extensively use eminent domain, principally exercising this power to create highways and obtain land for public buildings. In the early years the colonies compiled a checkered record with respect to the payment of compensation for land taken for roads. Several New England colonies and North Carolina commonly awarded compensation when any land was taken from its owners for a highway. Other colonies were more cavalier about invading property rights. South Carolina and Pennsylvania, for instance, awarded compensation only for taking improved or enclosed land. This practice, however, was not a denial of the compensation principle. Because land was plentiful, the colonists felt that unimproved land was of slight monetary value. Moreover, they reasoned that the advantages of a highway would more than offset the loss of a small amount of land by the owner.

As the colonies matured and land became more valuable, however, lawmakers increasingly acknowledged the right of landowners to receive compensation when the government took property. Thus, a 1765 New Jersey measure directed the award of compensation when land was appropriated for principal highways. Furthermore, compensation was regularly paid when colonial governments took land for the erection of buildings or large-scale projects other than highways. In Virginia, for instance, a landowner received compensation when his property was taken for the construction of the town of Suffolk. Similarly, New York statutes provided for payment when private land was used for the construction of wharves in New York City and the fortification of Schenectady.

During the colonial era the exercise of eminent domain was not limited by a narrow definition of the public purposes for which property could be taken. Anxious to foster economic growth, colonial lawmakers sometimes delegated the power of eminent domain to private individuals. Mill acts in many colonies authorized the proprietor of a gristmill to erect a dam and to flood the upper riparian owners' adjacent land. Compensation procedures varied, but the acts required mill operators either to pay damages or to institute a judicial proceeding to take the flooded land. In

Virginia the authority to take property was extended to fledgling industrial enterprises. A 1748 measure sought to encourage iron production by permitting the owner of an ironworks to cut down timber on adjacent land in order to maintain access roads. The ironworks owner was obligated to pay for such timber. Gristmills and manufacturing establishments, though privately owned, benefited the community and were viewed as types of public service. Hence, it was thought appropriate for such enterprises to possess the advantages of eminent domain.

Eminent domain was regularly employed in the colonies, but on a limited scale. Thus, the rights of property owners were not inviolate. Existing property arrangements were compelled to yield to the colony's social and economic needs. Moreover, colonial legislators broadly defined the nature of the public purpose that justified the exercise of eminent domain. The compensation principle, although recognized, was only imperfectly realized before the Revolution. Yet the colonists generally regarded just compensation as a fundamental principle. As undeveloped land gained in value, colonial lawmakers gradually abandoned the practice of taking without payment such land for roads. One scholar aptly observed that "the granting of compensation was well established and extensively practiced at and before the time of the Revolution."[13] The colonial experience with eminent domain set the stage for subsequent constitutional developments. Indeed, the compensation requirement was incorporated into the Fifth Amendment to the federal Constitution and became a constitutional norm safeguarding property ownership.

The constitutional underpinnings of property rights were forged during the colonial era. Blessed with abundant land, colonial America furnished a uniquely attractive environment for the property-conscious tenets of English constitutionalism. A substantial number of settlers could become landowners and improve their economic status, thereby strengthening the appeal of doctrines that enlarged the rights of property owners. The widespread ownership of land made the colonists especially sensitive to any interference with their property. By failing to respect the high value of property rights in the colonial mind, English imperial policy after 1763 precipitated the revolutionary crisis. Significantly, the cry "Liberty and Property" became the motto of the revolutionary movement.

2

The Revolutionary Era, 1765–1787

The American Revolution was preceded by more than a decade of political and intellectual ferment. Colonists vigorously debated such basic issues as the meaning of liberty and the nature of sovereignty. Throughout the revolutionary era, Americans emphasized the centrality of the right to property in constitutional thought. "The right of property," Arthur Lee of Virginia declared, "is the guardian of every other right, and to deprive a people of this, is in fact to deprive them of their liberty."[1] Hence, the protection of property ownership was an integral part of the American effort to fashion constitutional limits on governmental authority.

Yet thinking about property rights was more complex and contradictory than this would suggest. As is often the case, behavior did not always match professed belief. Moreover, the revolutionary period was characterized by a seeming paradox in American attitudes toward private property. One consequence of the revolutionary debates was a heightened concern for the protection of property rights. Revolutionary rhetoric and state constitutional provisions repeatedly linked liberty and property ownership. On the other hand, the revolutionary era saw widespread depredations of property held by both Loyalists and creditors. By the 1780s, many American leaders were bothered by this gap between the philosophical commitment to private property as a fundamental value in a free society and the infringement of these rights by state legislatures.

26

Ultimately their discomfort fueled the drive for a new form of government that would afford greater protection for property.

This keen concern about property rights in the revolutionary period is hardly surprising, because economic issues played an important role in shaping the movement for independence. Indeed, the defense of property rights was a major force unifying the colonies in their struggle with England. After 1763 the British Parliament sought to tighten imperial control over the American colonies, and this new policy had distinctly negative implications for American economic life. Stricter enforcement of the navigation acts threatened to curtail trading opportunities and was a major source of discontent. Even more menacing, however, were the persistent attempts by Parliament to tax the colonies. Maintaining that Parliament had no right to levy taxes on Americans, many colonists stressed the economic dimensions of liberty. The revolutionary slogan "No Taxation Without Representation" reflected the view that taxes imposed without consent were a type of confiscation that destroyed the right of property ownership. Thus, the Massachusetts Circular Letter of 1768 stated that "what a man has honestly acquired is absolutely his own, which he may freely give, but cannot be taken from him without his consent."[2]

In addition to the trading and taxation grievances, other colonial complaints also demonstrated the importance of property rights. Parliament's enactment of the Boston Port Bill, closing the harbor of that city, was viewed as an attack on the economic liberty of Bostonians and as an appropriation of private property. In 1774 members of Virginia's House of Burgesses condemned the Port Bill for depriving Bostonians "of their property, in wharfs erected by private persons, at their own great and proper expense, which act is, in our opinion, a most dangerous attempt to destroy the constitutional liberty and rights of North America."[3] Likewise, parliamentary attempts to enlarge the jurisdiction of admiralty courts posed a potential threat to maritime property and commerce. Because the admiralty courts functioned without a jury, it was easier for British officials to obtain convictions for violations of the trading acts. These revised admiralty procedures undercut the right to trial by jury, long regarded as an essential element of constitutional government. Mirroring community values, juries secured both liberty and property against the exercise of arbitrary power by crown officials. In 1766 the Delaware House of Assembly expressed this general sentiment by exalting trial by jury as "the great Preservative of public Liberty and private Property."[4]

Americans of the revolutionary era were particularly susceptible to political arguments stressing property rights. Easy availability of land had long characterized colonial society, and by the time of the revolutionary crisis the ownership of land was widespread. Indeed, this broad distribution of property was one of the most distinctive features of colonial life, in marked contrast with the situation in England. Even landless persons could reasonably hope to become owners eventually. Hence, the constitutional protection of economic liberty enjoyed great appeal.

American thinking about the constitutional significance of private property was in no sense original or distinctive. Clearly, the revolutionary attitude toward economic issues was partly molded by self-interested considerations. However, the colonial leaders drew heavily on the time-honored English Whig philosophy that regarded protection of private property as crucial to the preservation of freedom. According to Whig thought, property rights antedated political liberty. "In the eighteenth-century pantheon of British liberty," John Phillip Reid has pointed out, "there was no right more changeless and timeless than the right to property."[5] Economic issues had been at the forefront of the long struggle for political liberty in England. In 1775 Edmund Burke reminded Parliament "that the great contests for freedom in this country were from the earliest times chiefly upon the question of taxing."[6] Comparing the English and American experiences, colonial leaders simply demanded that English safeguards of property apply to the colonies.

Adhering to the English Whig tradition, colonial leaders viewed the security of property as the principal function of government. It followed that any government that rendered property rights insecure violated the very purpose of its existence. Such a government would forfeit the allegiance of its citizens and would be open to rebellion. By 1776 many Americans reluctantly came to believe that they could no longer remain in their colonial status and still enjoy constitutional protection of their rights. The English insistence on the sovereignty of Parliament clashed with older constitutional notions of natural rights and custom as restraints on arbitrary power. The Americans therefore declared their independence in the belief that they were defending their traditional rights under the English constitution against usurpation by Parliament and the Crown.

Designed to justify the Revolution, the Declaration of Independence illustrated this tie between political liberty and private property. Consistent with the Whig philosophy, the Declaration did not distinguish property from other natural rights. In drafting the Declaration, Thomas Jefferson borrowed heavily from the compact theory of John Locke. Locke used the expression "life, liberty, and estates" to describe the natural rights that government was formed to protect. Jefferson, however, substituted the phrase "pursuit of happiness" for "estates," a change that should not be understood as rejecting the emphasis on property rights in revolutionary ideology. The concept of happiness as an end of government was widely accepted in the eighteenth century and was generally equated with economic opportunity. As Willi Paul Adams noted, "The acquisition of property and the pursuit of happiness were so closely connected with each other in the minds of the founding generation that naming only one of the two sufficed to evoke both."[7] The right to obtain and possess property was at the heart of the pursuit of happiness. Still, Jefferson's formulation was significant because it stressed the importance of acquiring property rather than just the protection of existing property arrangements.

America's first national constitution, the Articles of Confederation, established a weak and decentralized government. Under the Articles, formally adopted in 1781, the states largely retained their sovereignty and independence. There was no executive branch, and the unicameral Continental Congress was granted only limited powers. Congress could not levy taxes and depended on requisitions among the states to obtain revenue. Amendment of the Articles required the unanimous consent of the state legislatures, which proved an insuperable barrier to reform proposals.

Despite these handicaps, Congress achieved some important legislative and administrative goals. Foremost among them was passage of the Northwest Ordinance in 1787. This measure established a system of government for the territory north of the Ohio River and furnished an important model for constitution drafting. Several provisions of the Northwest Ordinance concerned property rights. The ordinance also prohibited slavery, closing the area to one type of property. Other clauses contained safeguards for property ownership and contractual arrangements. In addition to declaring that no person should be deprived of liberty or property except "by the judgment of his peers or the law of the land,'' the Ordinance stated that if a person's property were taken for public purpose, "full compensation shall be made for the same.'' This was the first national legislation to incorporate the common law principle requiring compensation when government exercised the power of eminent domain. Further, the Ordinance provided that no law should "interfere with or affect private contracts, or engagements, *bona fide*, and without fraud, previously formed.'' In modified form, all three of these property guarantees found their way into the Constitution or the Bill of Rights.

Because the states remained substantially independent, the state constitutions were the key documents in determining Americans' rights and responsibilities. The Revolution initiated an era of innovation and constitutional experimentation by the states, as Americans debated what form their new governments should take. Because property ownership was associated with liberty and happiness, several of the first state constitutions included provisions to safeguard property rights. Drawing upon natural law principles, four state constitutions affirmed the freedom to obtain property. For example, the New Hampshire Constitution of 1784 stated: "All men have certain natural, essential, and inherent rights; among which are—the enjoying and defending life and liberty— acquiring, possessing and protecting property—and in a word, of seeking and obtaining happiness.'' Such right-to-acquire clauses not only proclaimed the protection of existing property rights but also enlarged economic opportunity for all citizens.

Echoing this prevalent commitment to economic liberty, the states acted to encourage the dispersal of wealth. Several state constitutions prohibited grants of monopoly; for example, the Maryland Constitution of 1776 declared that monopolies were "contrary to the spirit of a free government, and the principles of commerce.'' By either constitutional provision or statute most states abolished primogeniture and entail, devices that served to limit the inheritance of land to a single family heir. These practices were repugnant to many Americans, who saw them as symbols of the aristocratic land order they sought to escape. Reform of inheritance law increased owners' power to dispose of their land, but in practice operated to promote more widespread landownership among descendants.

The security of private property was also a matter of great concern to the framers of early state constitutions. Accordingly, the states placed specific guarantees of property rights in their constitutions. Property qualifications for both voters and officeholders were imposed. In language adopted from Magna Carta, the constitutions of five states, including Massachusetts and North Carolina, provided that no person could be "deprived of his life, liberty, or property but by the law of the land."

In a related development, there was an important shift with respect to the exercise of eminent domain power. Clauses in several state constitutions elevated to constitutional status the common law principle that compensation should be paid when private property was taken for public use. Although Vermont was not recognized as an independent state, the Vermont Constitution of 1777 was the first to adopt the compensation principle. The Massachusetts Constitution of 1780 followed suit, mandating that "whenever the public exigencies require that the property of any individual should be appropriated to public uses, he shall receive a reasonable compensation therefor." These confiscation provisions were forerunners of the takings clause of the Fifth Amendment. This move to constitutionalize the just compensation rule greatly strengthened the legal position of property owners.

Those states that did not adopt constitutional provisions requiring compensation often recognized the principle in legislation. Some jurisdictions halted the colonial practice of taking unimproved land for public roads without compensation. As urged by James Madison, Virginia lawmakers in 1785 for the first time required payment when unimproved land was taken for a roadway. Moreover, compensation clauses were invariably included in charters authorizing large-scale improvement projects. South Carolina, for instance, incorporated four canal companies in the 1780s, granting to each the power of eminent domain upon payment of compensation. Likewise, the Dismal Swamp Canal Company, created by Virginia in 1787, was authorized to take private land but was required to pay the owner the value of such property. Such state legislation was consistent with the just compensation clause of the Northwest Ordinance.

The broadly based nature of the desire to protect private property was strikingly illustrated by the Pennsylvania Constitution of 1776. The most radical of all state constitutions in the revolutionary era, Pennsylvania's constitution was designed to create an egalitarian society on the basis of popular sovereignty. For all its democratic features, however, the 1776

constitution included several provisions to safeguard property ownership. The charter placed "acquiring, possessing and protecting property" among the natural and inherent rights of all persons. The bitter
taxation controversy with England influenced the process of constitution
making. The Pennsylvania framers expressed the principle of no taxation
without representation, stipulating that "no part of a man's property can
be justly taken from him or applied to public uses, without his own
consent or that of his legal representatives." Another clause underscored
the importance assigned to trial by jury as a protection of property rights,
by asserting that "in controversies respecting property" the parties have
a right to a jury trial. Even more revealing, the Pennsylvania drafters
rejected a proposal to restrict the amount of property that an individual
could acquire. The framers of the Pennsylvania constitution attached a
high priority to property rights, viewing private property as fully consistent with the type of democratic society they wished to foster.

As this record indicates, the constitutional protection of property rights
was established in the states well before the adoption of the federal
Constitution. Indeed, the state experience with constitution making in the
revolutionary era strongly influenced the framing of the federal Constitution and the Bill of Rights. For example, state constitutional clauses
safeguarding persons against the deprivation of property "but by the law
of the land" imposed the equivalent of a due process requirement. This
concept was incorporated into the Fifth Amendment and became a
fundamental element of American constitutionalism.

In addition to constitutional guarantees of property rights, most of the
states expressly adopted English common law, unless repugnant to the
state constitution or unsuitable to American conditions, as the basis for
jurisprudence. This important step minimized legal upheaval and ensured
that continuity would be the hallmark of postrevolutionary administration
of justice. Continued reliance on English law meant that the conservative
and property-conscious tenets of common law would largely govern
private lawmaking. Ironically, the views of William Blackstone influenced American property law long after the break with England.

Although discussion of property rights primarily focused on such
traditional forms of wealth as land, slaves, and personalty, lawmakers
acted to recognize and protect intellectual property as well. In response to
a 1783 recommendation by the Continental Congress, every state enacted
legislation granting copyright protection to authors who were citizens of

the United States. Declaring that "the Security of literary Property must greatly tend to encourage Genius," North Carolina lawmakers recognized an author's exclusive privilege to publish books for a term of fourteen years. South Carolina's 1784 Act for the Encouragement of Arts and Sciences, which extended protection to inventions as well as literary property, was the first general patent law in American history. South Carolina and other states also issued special patents in the form of private acts. Notwithstanding widespread hostility to monopolies, lawmakers treated copyright and patent as special cases in which limited monopoly protection promoted the public interest by encouraging literary and mechanical innovation.

To newly independent Americans, respect for economic rights did not encompass unfettered liberty to use property in any manner. The theory of republicanism, influential during the revolutionary era, subordinated private interests to the pursuit of public welfare. As one historian observed, "The sacrifice of individual interests to the greater good of the whole formed the essence of republicanism."[8] Consequently, republicanism justified the regulation of private economic interests to promote the common good. The notion of the general welfare embodied in the republican ideal sometimes clashed with the rights of individual property owners and the growing ideology of a free-market economy.

Reflecting republican theory, both early state constitutions and revolutionary legislation limited the use of property in various ways. Asserting the primacy of public interest, the Vermont Constitution stated: "Private property ought to be subservient to public uses, when necessity requires it." Following the colonial practice, the Pennsylvania Constitution of 1776 guaranteed the right to hunt on unenclosed private land. This provision curtailed a landowner's exclusive dominion and marked a sharp departure from English land law. Furthermore, during the revolutionary war several states attempted to set the prices of goods and commodities. Regulation of public markets was also common. But such restrictions on the rights of property owners were not innovations; they only reflected the mercantilist assumptions of colonial economic policy.

Wartime necessity could also override private interest; for example, military operations sometimes required the destruction of property. Thus, in 1776 American forces burned a home in Charlestown, Massachusetts, to dislodge British troops. The owner, however, received no compensation for the loss. Congress consistently rejected such requests, reasoning that under the doctrine of necessity, persons were not entitled to indemnity when property was destroyed in combat with a hostile army. Similarly, local authorities lawfully seized and removed barrels of flour as the British army approached Philadelphia in 1777. Denying a reimbursement claim, the Supreme Court of Pennsylvania stressed the wartime conditions and observed that "it is better to suffer a private mischief, than a public inconvenience."[9]

An important reform emanating from the Revolution was the initial movement to abolish slavery, thereby eliminating this type of property. Of course, the Declaration of Independence contained no mention of emancipation, and many prominent slaveholders supported the patriot cause. Still, a growing number of Americans felt that slavery was a blemish on the republican ideal. During the revolutionary era, slavery was abolished in Pennsylvania and New England, never areas with a large servile population. As previously discussed, the Continental Congress prohibited slavery in the Northwest Territory. But this antislavery success was limited by a commitment to gradualism and respect for the property rights of masters. For example, Pennsylvania's 1780 emancipation statute applied only to the future generation of slaves, born after its effective date. Even then, the law postponed freedom until such slave children reached the age of twenty-eight, in order to reimburse their masters for the expenses of raising them. Although there was unmistakable progress toward the elimination of slavery, the process nonetheless emphasized the slaveholder's property interests.

On a more troublesome note, the Revolution also generated a wholesale interference with economic arrangements. Under well-settled principles of English common law, the property of traitors was subject to forfeiture. In 1777 the Continental Congress urged the states to seize property owned by Loyalists for the public benefit. This recommendation initiated a wave of confiscations from New Hampshire to Georgia. Relying on legislative power to punish traitors, state lawmakers enacted bills of attainder that declared named persons to be guilty of treason or the offense of adhering to the enemy. Persons so designated were banished, and all their real and personal property was confiscated. In Virginia, where Governor Thomas Jefferson was somewhat uneasy about a confiscation policy, the seizure of Loyalist property was achieved by legislation directed against enemy aliens rather than by a bill of attainder. A 1779 Virginia act declared that British subjects were incapable of holding real and personal property, and that such property was vested in the state. Vast amounts of land were forfeited pursuant to these statutes. Roger Morris of New York, for instance, lost fifty thousand acres, and Henry McCulloch of North Carolina forfeited more than sixty thousand acres. Typically the confiscated property was vested in state commissioners, who were charged with selling the property at public auction. In an effort to prevent land monopolies and to encourage a wide distribution of property, the commissioners were required to divide the land into tracts of not more than five hundred acres. Confiscation thus served the dual purpose of punishing the Loyalists and producing revenue to finance the war. Some states, such as New York, profited greatly by their seizures. For Georgia, on the other hand, the confiscation of Loyalist estates produced only a meager return. Further, it is unclear that the confiscation and sale of Loyalist property resulted in any significant redistribution of land to poorer persons.

Debts owed to British merchants were another target of the state legislatures. Because tobacco planters in Virginia had incurred large personal obligations, lawmakers in the Old Dominion were especially active in fashioning legal obstacles to the recovery of British debts. In 1777 the legislature appropriated all debts owed to British subjects. Virginians were authorized to pay the state what they owed and to obtain a discharge of their indebtedness. This sequestration scheme was designed to raise money for the state treasury at the expense of enemy aliens. Moreover, Virginians closed their courts to suits by British creditors. Debtors in the Old Dominion took advantage of these arrangements to eliminate a substantial part of their personal obligations. Similar legislation hampered the recovery of debts in North Carolina and Maryland.

The cessation of hostilities in 1783 did not bring much solace to Loyalists whose property was confiscated or to British creditors. The Treaty of Paris provided that there should be no further seizures of property. Many states, however, disregarded this obligation, and the confiscation of Loyalist property continued; indeed, North Carolina seized Loyalist land as late as 1790. With respect to already confiscated property, the Treaty merely required Congress to recommend that state legislatures make restitution of forfeited estates. As might be expected, the states ignored such recommendations. Lawsuits by Loyalist claimants in both state and federal courts proved fruitless. In *Cooper v. Telfair*

(1800) Justice William Cushing observed: "The right to confiscate and banish, in the case of an offending citizen, must belong to every government."[10] Consequently, most Loyalists never received any compensation for their property from the states.

On paper British merchants fared somewhat better, as the Treaty stated that creditors "shall meet with no lawful Impediment to the Recovery of the full value" of all previous debts. In actuality many Americans continued to resist paying their obligations. Eventually the Supreme Court, in *Ware v. Hylton* (1796), held that the Treaty provision concerning creditors superseded Virginia's sequestration statute. Only under prodding by federal courts during the 1790s did British creditors recover even a fraction of what they were owed.

Confiscation and sequestration were highly popular wartime measures, but the implications of such laws were disquieting to some prominent legal and political figures. Widespread seizure of Loyalist property did not bode well for the security of property rights, and unpaid British debts endangered commercial credit abroad. Hoping to rehabilitate former Loyalists, John Adams, John Jay, and Patrick Henry urged leniency and worked to moderate confiscation policy. In 1784 James Madison successfully sponsored a bill to halt further confiscation of British property in Virginia. Many political figures felt that continued harsh treatment of Loyalists alienated useful persons and discouraged the revival of trade. In *Rutgers v. Waddington* (1784) Alexander Hamilton represented a British merchant in a challenge to New York's Trespass Act, which gave patriots a cause of action for use of their abandoned land by the British during their occupation of New York City. Hamilton skillfully argued that the statute was contrary to the law of nations and the Treaty of Paris. He secured a partial victory when the Mayor's Court restricted the reach of the Trespass Act and held that the legislature could not have intended to violate the law of nations. As anti-Loyalist feeling gradually subsided, state lawmakers relieved some persons from confiscation.

Unlike many other states, South Carolina generally adopted a conservative posture toward wartime confiscation and the payment of English debts. Lawmakers were particularly generous in granting petitions for relief from the property seizure statutes. Wives and widows of Loyalists, for example, were often successful in recovering their husbands' property. Moreover, the South Carolina courts held that a widow was entitled to dower in her late husband's land that had been sold under the confiscation acts. Courts in South Carolina also were sympathetic to the claims of English creditors seeking to collect prerevolutionary debts. One scholar found that "South Carolina judges preferred the strict performance of contractual undertakings to the satisfactions of revenge against British merchants or Loyalist refugees."[11]

Loyalists and British citizens were not the only ones whose property rights were attacked. In response to depressed economic conditions during the postrevolutionary period, state lawmakers often paid little heed to abstract considerations of property rights. They turned instead to debtor-relief laws and the issuance of paper money, measures designed to aid debtors at the expense of creditors. State legislatures repeatedly intervened in debtor–creditor relations with a host of laws staying executions for debts, permitting the payment of obligations in installments, and making depreciated paper currency legal tender. Rhode Island's paper-money scheme, requiring creditors to accept almost valueless currency, was especially egregious. Another notorious measure was South Carolina's Pine Barren Act of 1785, which permitted debtors to tender distant property or worthless pineland in discharge of their obligations. Creditors and merchants viewed such laws as simply a confiscation of their wealth by fraudulent means. James Madison, for example, opposed the issuance of paper currency in Virginia, warning that paper money "affects Rights of property as much as taking away equal value in land."[12]

In a similar vein, the Pennsylvania legislature in 1785, at the behest of radicals and agrarians, revoked the corporate charter of the Bank of North America. The first incorporated bank in the United States, the Bank of North America received charters from both the Continental Congress and Pennsylvania. This repeal undid the action of a previous legislative session and sparked a bitter debate. Critics charged that the Bank promoted the accumulation of wealth, hampered the circulation of paper money, and was incompatible with democratic government. James Wilson, later a member of the constitutional convention, defended the Bank and argued against the annulment of the state charter. He contended that the act chartering the Bank constituted a contract between the state and the corporation that Pennsylvania was bound to respect. Wilson maintained that "while these terms are observed on one side, the compact cannot, consistently with the rules of good faith, be departed from on the other.''[13] The view that corporate charters were contracts not subject to legislative revocation anticipated subsequent jurisprudence but did not carry the day in the political climate of 1785. To conservatives the repeal of the Bank's charter was further evidence that state governments could not be relied on to respect property rights.

State constitutional provisions to safeguard property proved ineffective against this legislative onslaught. During the postrevolutionary period, state courts occasionally tried to protect the interests of creditors against legislative interference with contractual arrangements, but they were unable to prevail in the face of popular majorities. Judicial impotence was dramatically illustrated in *Trevett v. Weeden* (1786), a case involving Rhode Island's controversial paper-money scheme. At issue was a proceeding instituted by a private party on behalf of the state against a butcher who declined to sell meat for depreciated paper money. His refusal violated a penal law imposing a fine on persons refusing paper money at face value. Apparently relying on the colonial charter, counsel for the defendant argued that the penal statute enforcing the legal tender law, which provided for a trial without a jury or the right of appeal, was unconstitutional. Although the Supreme Court of Rhode Island rendered no formal opinion about the constitutional issue, several judges expressed the view that the penal law was "repugnant and unconstitutional." The court unanimously dismissed the complaint. Furious legislators censured the court and debated a proposal to remove the judges. Such excesses support Forrest McDonald's conclusion that "Americans were not as secure in their property rights between 1776 and 1787 as they had been during the colonial period."[14] Not surprisingly, conservatives grew alarmed about legislative redistribution of wealth and became increasingly convinced that the state governments were unable to protect economic rights.

Despoliation of property rights was not the only economic woe that confronted Americans following independence. Business conditions were chaotic, and the states quarreled constantly over trade matters. The states were virtually independent under the Articles of Confederation, and the national government was powerless to control the economy, provide for the public debt, or compel compliance with the Treaty of Paris. Commercial rivalry among the states threatened to destroy any semblance of union and made national policy impossible. With no control over commerce, Congress found it difficult to negotiate commercial treaties with foreign governments. States levied tariff duties on goods transported from other states, frustrating attempts to promote interstate trade. Those states with good ports, such as New York, placed export duties on goods shipped overseas from sister jurisdictions. A generation later Chief Justice John Marshall questioned whether anything contributed more to the adoption of the Constitution "than the deep and general conviction that commerce ought to be regulated by Congress."[15]

Also bothersome was the lack of congressional authority to levy taxes. Requisitions on the states were often unpaid, and the financial condition of the national government became critical. Unable to raise adequate revenue to redeem the war debt, Congress resorted to the emission of unsecured paper currency. Inflation raged unchecked, inflicting substantial losses on persons holding paper money. This fiscal embarrassment undermined the ability of Congress to secure further credit. Disputes over public finance dominated the political agenda of the Confederation period and highlighted the broad divisions in American society between mercantile interests and agrarians.

The heated struggle between debtors and creditors raised the specter of domestic insurrection. Indebtedness bore heavily on farmers, and forcible resistance to the collection of debts spread in rural areas. In April 1785 an unruly crowd intimidated jurors and prevented Judge John F. Grimke from trying debt cases in Camden, South Carolina. Similar disturbances took place elsewhere across the state. New Jersey and Virginia also experienced violent agrarian protests against judicial proceedings to collect debts.

A more serious outbreak, known as Shays's Rebellion, occurred in western Massachusetts during the fall and winter of 1786–87. Protesting high taxes and a depressed economy, farmers petitioned the state government to issue paper money, which would ease the payment of debts. Many farmers feared foreclosure or imprisonment for debt as merchants pressed to collect unpaid obligations. The refusal of Massachusetts lawmakers to enact a paper-money scheme sparked protest directed against lawyers, the court system, and the collection of debts. Bands of farmers closed the courts in the western portion of the state and prevented the execution of judgments against debtors. By threat of force, the Shaysites thus achieved temporary relief for indebted farmers.

Merchants and creditors in eastern Massachusetts viewed these events with horror. They saw the disruption of the courts as undermining contractual obligations, rendering property rights insecure, and portending anarchy. In actuality, most Shaysites owned small farms and never envisioned the abolition of private property. Exaggerated accounts of the size and radical aims of Shays's Rebellion, however, were circulated in other states, alarming conservatives with fears of property redistribution. John Marshall, for instance, worried that the Shaysite troubles "cast a deep shade over that bright prospect which the revolution in America and the establishment of our free governments had opened to the votaries of liberty throughout the globe."[16] Congress lacked sufficient power to handle this crisis, but after several months the governor of Massachusetts raised a private army and dispersed Shays's insurgents. Although Shays's Rebellion failed to achieve any long-range objectives, it created a crisis atmosphere and accelerated the movement to frame a new constitution. Inadvertently the Shaysites convinced many political leaders that a stronger national government was necessary.

The initial moves toward calling a constitutional convention were made in January 1786. Virginia's legislature invited other states to name commissioners who would meet "to take into consideration the trade of the United States." This commercial convention was held in September in Annapolis, Maryland. Only five states—Virginia, Delaware, Pennsylvania, New Jersey, and New York—were represented at the Annapolis convention. Under the circumstances it was impossible to conduct any substantive business. But following the leadership of Alexander Hamilton and James Madison, the commissioners seized the opportunity to call for more effective government. Decrying "the embarrassments which characterise the present State of our national affairs," the Annapolis convention unanimously urged another meeting of state representatives "to devise such further provisions as shall appear to them necessary to render the constitution of the Federal Government adequate to the exigencies of the Union."[17] The meeting was scheduled for Philadelphia in May 1787.

At first this recommendation for another meeting was largely ignored, but news of Shays's Rebellion played a crucial role in marshaling support for the Philadelphia convention. Frightened by the prospect of domestic turmoil, many state legislatures appointed delegates to the Philadelphia meeting during the most threatening months of the Shaysite insurgency. Then in February 1787 the Continental Congress belatedly adopted a resolution supporting the convention. Thus, the stage was set for a constitutional convention that, among other concerns, would seek to safeguard property rights and create the legal framework for commercial expansion.

The dissolution of political ties with England compelled Americans to make fundamental decisions about the nature of their new republican society. Influenced by the Whig political tradition as well as English common law, colonial leaders assigned property rights an essential place in the evolution of revolutionary constitutionalism. English policies that threatened colonial economic interests served to strengthen the philosophical link between property ownership and the enjoyment of political liberty. Accordingly, it was entirely logical that the right to property was among the highest social values in the new republic. Early state constitutions emphasized the legal protection of property rights. One scholar has aptly concluded that "the sanctity of private property was central to the new American social and political order."[18]

Despite this exaltation of property rights as part of the revolutionary ideology, experience soon demonstrated that state safeguards for property were inadequate. Although there was no retreat from the formal commitment to property rights, state legislatures repeatedly interfered with the rights of property owners. Sweeping confiscation and sequestration measures were directed against Loyalists and British merchants. The issuance of paper money and the passage of debtor-relief laws benefited agrarians at the expense of the mercantile community. To compound this insecurity of property, economic relations were badly dislocated once independence was obtained. The states carried on destructive trade wars against one another. Congress was powerless to deal effectively with this problem. By 1787 many political leaders were convinced that only a more energetic national government could sufficiently protect property ownership, regulate commerce, and restore public credit. Ironically, the assaults on property rights during the Confederation period stimulated greater constitutional safeguards for property holders.

3

"Property Must Be Secured":
Establishing a
New Constitutional Order

The Philadelphia convention was a watershed in the evolution of American constitutionalism. After deliberating from May to September 1787 the delegates ultimately proposed a new form of government to replace the Articles of Confederation. Much has been written about the differences among the convention delegates and the need for compromises. Particularly nettlesome were the questions of representation in the legislative branch and the amount of executive power. Nonetheless, there was a large measure of consensus among the framers. Most favored a more vigorous national government that could protect property rights, promote commerce, establish credit by paying the public debt, and suppress insurrection. Rather than chronicling the events of the constitutional convention and ratification campaign, this chapter examines the extent to which property and economic issues shaped the process of constitution making.

The delegates to the constitutional convention were an able and experienced group, most of whom had participated in public affairs during the revolutionary era. Harboring little faith in the people, the framers were not democrats in any modern sense. Indeed, they viewed popular government as a potential threat to property rights. The convention debates were conducted at a high intellectual level. Dominated by northern merchants, southern planters, and lawyers, the delegates for the most part were wealthy individuals. This fact has caused some historians to contend that the framers' property-conscious attitude reflected their economic self-interest. Although one can never entirely dismiss economic motives, such an analysis seems unduly simplistic, as it does not give enough attention to the philosophical climate that helped define the framers' constitutional outlook. The doctrine that property ownership was essential for the enjoyment of liberty had long been a fundamental tenet of Anglo-American constitutional thought. Moreover, the framers represented diverse and potentially antagonistic interests. Some feared a conflict between the rich and the poor, whereas others foresaw a division between mercantile and agricultural interests. They were by no means in agreement on the full range of economic matters before the convention.

Despite their differences over particular economic issues, the right to acquire and own property was undoubtedly a paramount value for the framers of the Constitution. Following the Lockean philosophy, John Rutledge of South Carolina advised the Philadelphia convention that "Property was certainly the principal object of Society."[1] Similarly, Alexander Hamilton declared: "One great objt. of Govt. is personal protection and the security of Property."[2] These sentiments were widely shared by other delegates. Consistent with the Whig tradition, the framers did not distinguish between personal and property rights. On the contrary, in their minds, property rights were indispensable because property ownership was closely associated with liberty. "Property must be secured," John Adams proclaimed in 1790, "or liberty cannot exist."[3] Indeed, the framers saw property ownership as a buffer protecting individuals from governmental coercion. Arbitrary redistributions of property destroyed liberty, and thus the framers hoped to restrain attacks on property rights.

Accordingly, many provisions of the Constitution pertain to property interests and were designed to rectify the abuses that characterized the revolutionary era. These clauses fall into four general categories. The first group of provisions restricted the power of the new national government with respect to property and economic activity. Thus, the Constitution prohibited Congress from enacting bills of attainder or from declaring a forfeiture of property for treason except during the life of the offender. Mindful of the destructive commercial rivalry among the states over foreign trade, Congress was forbidden to give preferential treatment to the port of any state. The delegates from the lower South, which produced staple crops for foreign markets, secured a ban on the levy of export duties by Congress. Finally, the Constitution denied Congress the authority to impose direct taxes unless apportioned according to population. As a practical matter, this requirement greatly limited the power of Congress to levy land taxes and capitulation or head taxes. In effect it shielded landed wealth from federal taxation.

Another cluster of provisions was intended to strengthen the hand of the national government over economic matters. Aside from the constraints just noted, the Constitution granted Congress broad powers of taxation. This move gave Congress the authority to generate sufficient revenue to assume payment of the outstanding war debt and thereby to improve American access to foreign credit markets. It also meant that Congress could use its taxing power to encourage economic growth through protective tariffs. Equally important was the authority vested in Congress to regulate interstate and foreign commerce. A direct response to state interference with trade, the commerce clause guaranteed that the United States would enjoy the benefits of a national market for goods.

Additional powers of Congress concerning property also warrant attention. In recognition of the emerging importance of intellectual property, the Constitution vested Congress with authority to award copyrights and patents to authors and inventors. Another commercially significant clause gave Congress the power "to establish uniform laws on the Subject of Bankruptcy throughout the United States." Although the constitutional convention gave little attention to this clause, the framers likely thought of bankruptcy in connection with the regulation of commerce. They anticipated that a bankruptcy law would operate largely for the benefit of merchants and traders, as was the practice in England, and would protect creditors from fraudulent debtors.

The third set of provisions placed restrictions on the power of the states. To conservatives the experience of the revolutionary period demonstrated that the state governments could not be trusted to respect property rights. A principal objective of the framers was to prevent the state legislatures from redistributing property. The Constitution freed foreign and interstate commerce from state taxation by banning state taxes on imports and exports. In reaction to the wave of Loyalist property confiscations during the revolutionary era, the states were prevented from enacting bills of attainder. Recalling the bitter controversies over state legal tender statutes, the framers prohibited the states from issuing bills of credit or making anything but gold or silver coin legal tender for the payment of debts.

Foremost among the constitutional limitations on state authority was the provision forbidding the states from enacting any law "impairing the obligation of contracts." In time the contract clause became one of the most significant parts of the Constitution. Yet there was surprisingly little discussion of this clause at the constitutional convention. The initial proposal for a contract clause, modeled closely on the Northwest Ordinance, called for a prohibition on state interference with private contracts. The reaction of the convention was cool, however, with several delegates objecting that the proposed restriction would unduly intrude into state jurisdiction. Nonetheless, the committee on style, which prepared the final document, included the contract clause in the Constitution. The authorship of the clause remains uncertain, but historians have asserted that either Alexander Hamilton or James Wilson was the likely drafter.

There has long been dispute about the scope of the contract clause. It seems apparent that the clause was immediately directed against state debtor-relief legislation, which assisted debtors at the expense of creditors. An important question, however, was whether the restriction applied only to contracts between private individuals or whether it extended to contracts made by state governments. Although some scholars have argued that the framers intended a narrow construction of the contract clause, there is no evidence that the framers drew a sharp distinction between public and private contracts. Indeed, there is some basis for a broad interpretation of the contract clause. As noted earlier, in 1785 James Wilson forcefully maintained that an act chartering a corporation constituted a contract between the state and the corporation. Hence, the corporation's charter was not subject to legislative revocation. Moreover, the language of the clause as adopted is more comprehensive than that of the initial proposal because it is not limited to private contracts. The thinking of the framers may never be ascertained with certainty, but there is historical evidence that the prohibition of the clause protected both public and private contracts against impairment.

The fourth category of provisions was concerned with the protection of slave property. No other type of property received such detailed attention from the framers. Slavery had existed in colonial America since the early seventeenth century and was legally recognized everywhere before the revolutionary era. Furthermore, much of the wealth in the southern states rested on slave labor. Viewing slavery as a settled part of the social order, the delegates to the Philadelphia convention never considered the abolition of human bondage. Such a move not only would have been impossible to implement but also would surely have caused the collapse of the convention. Nonetheless, many delegates shared a tepid antislavery sentiment that occasionally surfaced in the debates.

Spearheaded by South Carolina, the delegates from the lower South worked steadily to secure constitutional safeguards for slave property.[4] Fearing that the new national government might encroach on slavery, southerners demanded the adoption of clauses to buttress the institution of slavery. During the convention, southern delegates employed threats of disunion to force important concessions on the slavery issue. Despite the commercial orientation of many delegates, the convention eventually accepted three key provisions favorable to the agricultural interests of the South. Following a bitter debate over the importation of slaves from abroad, Congress was denied the authority to prohibit the slave trade until 1808. The rendition of escaped slaves was also a priority for southerners. Accordingly, the fugitive slave clause declared that persons held to service or labor under state law ''shall be delivered up on Claim of the Party to whom such Service or Labour may be due.'' Southern delegates also wanted slaves to be counted as free persons for the purpose of apportioning seats in the House of Representatives, but they were forced to accept a compromise under which three fifths of the slave population was so tallied. The three-fifths clause guaranteed additional political clout for slave states in the House. One historian has aptly pointed out that ''slavery was more clearly and explicitly established under the Constitution than it had been under the Articles.''[5] The slavery clauses set the stage for acrimonious sectional conflict in future years, but as James Madison acknowledged, agreement on these provisions was essential to gain southern support for the Constitution.

Although numerous clauses in the Constitution deal with specific economic interests, they contain no language that broadly affirmed the right of property. Unlike many of the early state constitutions, the federal Constitution did not proclaim the natural right of property ownership or declare that a person could not be deprived of property except by due process of law. These striking omissions, however, may be understood by taking into account the larger political considerations that guided the deliberations of the constitutional convention.

For all their devotion to property rights, the framers were content to rely primarily on institutional and political arrangements to safeguard property owners. The basic constitutional scheme was to protect individual rights, including property, by limiting the exercise of government power through elaborate procedural devices. The framers expected that the separation of powers among the branches of the federal government would create a political climate of checks and balances in which property interests would be safe. Believing that unrestrained democracy posed a threat to liberty and property, the framers looked to the strong executive and the independent judiciary as curbs on legislative interference with property rights. Extolling the separation of powers, John Adams later explained: "The great art of lawgiving consists in balancing the poor against the rich in the legislature, and in constituting the legislative a perfect balance against the executive power. . . . The essence of a free government consists in an effectual control of rivalries."[6]

Further, the framers anticipated that property owners would dominate the new government and that such persons could be relied on to respect property rights. Hamilton, for instance, predicted that Congress would be largely composed of "landholders, merchants, and men of the learned professions."[7] Under English law, participation in political affairs had long been confined to property owners, and a few delegates favored establishing a property requirement for suffrage and membership in Congress. It proved difficult, however, to formulate uniform standards. Accordingly, the Constitution allowed the states to determine the qualifications for voting. When the Constitution was written, virtually every state imposed a property or taxpaying qualification on suffrage and set higher property qualifications to hold public office. The framers in effect accepted such state-imposed criteria for participation in national elections. They failed to foresee the rapid emergence of universal manhood suffrage in the early nineteenth century, a move that would upset their calculations.

Lastly, the Constitution as originally drafted did not contain a bill of rights to guarantee individual liberty. The framers deliberately decided not to frame a declaration of rights because they deemed it unnecessary to restrain a government of limited powers. Further, they felt that the states' bills of rights offered adequate protection to individuals. In their view there was no reason to identify any protected liberties, including the rights of property ownership.

The constitutional principle of federalism also had important implications for economic rights. The framers in effect divided power between the federal and the state governments by erecting a new national government over the existing states. Because the federal government could exercise only enumerated powers, the states retained general legislative authority. The Constitution placed certain constraints on state authority, but within broad limits the states could promote and regulate economic activity. In addition, the states could enact statutes governing the health, safety, and morals of their citizens, although such laws often curtailed the use of property. Until the twentieth century the states remained the principal source of laws regulating land use and business enterprise. Under the doctrine of federalism the states enjoyed great latitude in governing economic activity, but the boundary between federal and state authority was indistinct. Much state economic regulation was challenged as interfering with interstate commerce or infringing on constitutionally protected property rights. As a result, there was frequent tension between property-conscious federal judges and state legislatures.

Consistent with the republican notion that political authority rested on popular consent, the framers submitted the Constitution for ratification by popularly elected state conventions. The ensuing ratification debate of 1787–88 produced the first organized political contest in American history. Proponents of the Constitution called themselves Federalists and labeled critics of the Constitution as Anti-Federalists. Most of the delegates to the constitutional convention signed the new instrument of government and used their considerable influence to secure approval. As part of the campaign to win ratification in New York, James Madison, Alexander Hamilton, and John Jay composed *The Federalist,* a series of newspaper essays that skillfully explained the provisions of the Constitution and the philosophy on which the fundamental law was based.

The Federalist attachment to property went beyond the philosopical position that property constituted the basis of civil society and a safeguard of liberty. Federalists also emphasized the economic utility of private property. In their view, a strong national economy rested on private ownership. Security of property and respect for contractual arrangements facilitated the development of investment capital, a crucial feature of a commercial society. "Federalists proposed, in sum," one scholar has concluded, "to place the new land in the mainstream of acquisitive capitalism."[8] This market economy would generate additional wealth and ultimately benefit all citizens of the new republic through increased services and goods.

Consequently, economic reform was a major Federalist priority. Supporters of the Constitution blamed inadequate government under the Articles for loss of credit, lower land values, and decay of commerce during the 1780s. Throughout the ratification debates the Federalists stressed the economic advantages of a strong central government. They argued that ratification of the Constitution would facilitate the restoration of credit and would encourage commerce and manufacturing. Downplaying differences between agricultural and mercantile interests, proponents stressed the mutuality of economic activity and linked commercial growth with enhanced land values. The Federalists also maintained that under the Constitution the United States could more effectively protect American interests overseas.

In addition to improving commerce, proponents of the Constitution argued that the new government would better safeguard property ownership. In his famous tenth *Federalist* essay Madison observed that the right of property derived from "diversity in the faculties of men." Echoing sentiments expressed at the constitutional convention, he added that the "protection of these faculties is the first object of government." Recognizing that "the most common and durable source of factions had been the various and unequal distribution of property," Madison contended that economic factions would inevitably clash in Congress. The public good would be served, however, by enlarging the sphere of government, as it would be more difficult for any special-interest group to gain control and invade the rights of others. "A rage for paper money, for an abolition of debts, for an equal division of property, or for any other improper and wicked project," Madison asserted, "will be less apt to pervade the whole body of the Union than a particular member of it."[9] In short, extended representation would diffuse the tendency of majority factions at the state level to oppress the minority, particularly property owners.

Often linked together for the purpose of discussion, the various restrictions on state power to impair contracts and issue paper money contained in Article I, Section 10, were presented as additional protections of commerce and property rights. Writing in *The Federalist*,

Hamilton praised "the precautions against the repetition of those practices on the part of the state governments, which have undermined the foundations of property and credit."[10] Similarly, Charles Pinckney of South Carolina considered this section to be "the soul of the Constitution." He expected that these limitations on the states would restore American credit in foreign markets: "No more shall paper money, no more shall tender-laws, drive their commerce from our shores, and darken the American name in every country where it is known."[11]

The contract clause by itself did not prompt much discussion during the ratification debates. Speaking in broad terms, Madison declared that "laws impairing the obligation of contracts, are contrary to the first principles of the social compact, and to every principle of sound legislation." Moreover, he described the contract clause as a "bulwark in favor of personal security and private rights."[12] Other Federalists explained the provision in terms of state debtor-relief legislation. Thus, David Ramsay of South Carolina observed that the contract clause and prohibition of state paper money "will doubtless bear hard on debtors who wish to defraud their creditors, but it will be real service to the honest part of the community."[13] These brief remarks cast little light on the application of the clause to public contracts. William R. Davie of North Carolina stated that the clause "refers merely to contracts between individuals," but he was the only proponent of the Constitution to adopt a narrow construction.[14]

Several Federalists expressed the view that the limitations on state power found in Article I, Section 10, generated much of the opposition to the Constitution. But there is little evidence to support this position with respect to the contract clause. In fact, opponents of the Constitution rarely focused on the contract clause in urging rejection of the proposed new government. A few Anti-Federalists, however, warned that the clause could have a broad application. Luther Martin of Maryland perceived that this provision would have a sweeping impact on debtor-relief legislation. Rejecting the notion that contracts should be protected under every circumstance, he asserted that in "times of such *great public calamities* and *distress*" state governments should have the power to assist debtors. The contract clause, Martin feared, would curtail state authority "to prevent the *wealthy creditor* and the *monied man* from *totally* destroying the *poor* though even *industrious* debtor."[15] At the Virginia ratifying convention Patrick Henry went a step further, prophetically asserting that the provision "includes public contracts, as well as private contracts between individuals."[16] Significantly, no Federalist disputed Henry's interpretation of the clause.

Another source of concern regarding the Constitution was sensitivity for the economic position of debtors. At least some Anti-Federalists worried that the new scheme of government would prove beneficial to creditors and increase the hardship of debtors. Particularly in the southern states, the Anti-Federalists warned that the creation of a federal court system would facilitate the collection of old debts owed to British merchants.

Despite infrequent references to the contract clause or the plight of debtors, the Anti-Federalist critique was remarkable for its omission of any sustained attention to economic issues. Few critics of the Constitution, for instance, openly defended the issuance of paper money by the states. Anti-Federalists advanced numerous complaints about the proposed Constitution, but they rarely attacked the specific provisions related to property interests. To be sure, opponents repeatedly charged that the new form of government would benefit the wealthy and foster aristocracy. Such general comments were directed against the entire constitutional scheme and reflected fear of elite political control rather than fundamental disagreement over property rights and economic liberty. Indeed, the leading Anti-Federalists were landowners who shared the prevailing view that respect for property was an essential element of republicanism.

In the southern states some large slaveholders joined the ranks of the Anti-Federalists. Opponents of the Constitution, therefore, were quick to raise the sensitive issue of slave property. Anti-Federalists argued that the Constitution afforded inadequate protection to slavery. They were particularly agitated that Congress had the power to halt the importation of slaves in 1808. Somewhat defensively, Charles C. Pinckney of South Carolina, a leading Federalist, explained that "considering all the circumstances, we have made the best terms for the security of this species of property it was in our power to make."[17]

The most compelling objection to ratification concerned the lack of a bill of rights. Above all, the Anti-Federalists were distrustful of consolidated national power which seemingly threatened the authority of the states as well as individual liberty. They demanded express assurances to safeguard rights against federal authority. Accordingly, in the state ratifying conventions, opponents of the Constitution pressed for a federal bill of rights to preserve state power and personal rights from impairment by the new government. Massachusetts, which ratified the Constitution in February 1788, was the first of several states to recommend amendments to "guard against an undue administration of the federal government."[18] Such requests for a bill of rights were adopted by four other states. Anxious to win support for the Constitution, the Federalists informally agreed to accept a bill of rights as the price of ratification. This tactical concession proved crucial to gaining acceptance of the Constitution in closely divided states, such as Virginia and New York.

Although the ratification debates turned primarily on political and constitutional issues rather than economic questions, public attitudes in many states reflected socioeconomic divisions. This split was largely along commercial lines. Persons involved in the market economy were likely to favor the Constitution. Hence, the Federalists represented the learned professions, merchants, creditors, and planters who were producing crops for export. Their intellectual horizons were enlarged by education and international trade. Federalist support was concentrated in cities and the Atlantic seaboard. Anti-Federalists, on the other hand, spoke for small farmers, debtors, and backcountry residents less involved with commercial activity. These groups possessed a predominantly local economic outlook focused on agriculture. They enjoyed fewer educational advantages and often resided away from lines of communication. Because many Anti-Federalists lived at the fringe of the market economy, they anticipated few advantages from improved commerce. On the contrary, the Anti-Federalists feared that the federal government would levy heavy taxes and favor mercantile interests.

This evidence of class division lends some support to an economic interpretation of the Constitution. One must be careful, however, not to exaggerate the economic dimensions of the constitution-making process. As we have seen, economic issues did not figure prominently in the ratification debates. Certainly no political leader questioned the right to hold private property. With respect to economic matters, the difference between the Federalists and the Anti-Federalists was limited to whether the new federal government or the states were more appropriate to govern commerce and protect property.

During the first Congress, Madison, as a representative from Virginia, took the initiative in redeeming the Federalists' belated promise to propose a bill of rights. Despite continued misgivings by some Federalists about the need for a bill of rights, Madison prepared a series of constitutional amendments based largely on the proposals of the state ratifying conventions. In formulating these amendments he was careful to avoid controversial innovations and to preserve the effectiveness of the new federal government. For the most part Madison incorporated traditional guarantees already recognized in state bills of rights or English common law. The process of drafting the Bill of Rights was thus substantially derivative in nature.

Apparently reasoning that the federal government was unlikely to threaten property ownership, the proposals adopted by the state ratifying conventions demonstrated little concern for property rights. Only Virginia and North Carolina called for specific property safeguards. Both state conventions requested a declaration that "the means of acquiring, possessing, and protecting property" was among the unalienable natural rights of the people. Virginians and North Carolinians also urged adoption of an amendment providing that no person should be "deprived of his life, liberty, or property, but by the law of the land."[19] These proposals merely confirmed prevailing constitutional thought. As we have seen, several state constitutions already characterized property as a natural right and contained a due process guarantee.

The state ratifying conventions, however, revealed a widespread commitment to free trade and economic opportunity. Four states recommended a prohibition of monopolies. The Massachusetts convention, for example, called for an amendment that "Congress erect no company of merchants with exclusive advantages of commerce."[20] Similarly, Thomas Jefferson urged Madison to seek an amendment restricting monopolies. Already prohibited by two state constitutions, monopolies were perceived as a blatant infringement on the property rights of others to engage in business. Although Madison did not include a ban on monopolies in the proposed bill of rights, this dislike of exclusive economic privilege long influenced American constitutional thought.

Given Madison's long record as a champion of property rights, it could hardly have been a surprise that he included protection for property owners in the proposed bill of rights. Moreover, Madison was privately uneasy about the future security of property. The original Constitution placed few specific restrictions on the federal government in order to guarantee property rights. Madison envisioned a time when property owners might constitute a vulnerable minority under the political control of the majority. Fearing that majority rule might not provide adequate protection for property owners, he sought to strengthen the constitutional guarantees of property. In language reminiscent of several state constitutions, Madison suggested attaching to the Constitution a broad statement of political theory that encompassed property ownership: "That government is instituted, and ought to be exercised for the benefit of the people; which consists in the enjoyment of life and liberty, with the right of acquiring and using property, and generally of pursuing and obtaining happiness and safety."[21] Perhaps thinking that the purposes of government were self-evident, Congress did not accept this declaration.

Madison was more successful in gaining approval of his other property-related proposals. As finally adopted, the Fifth Amendment contains two important property guarantees, along with procedural safeguards governing criminal trials. The amendment provides in part that no person shall be "deprived of life, liberty, or property, without due process of law; nor shall private property be taken for public use, without just compensation." Madison's decision to place this language next to criminal justice protections, such as the prohibitions against double jeopardy and self-incrimination, underscored the close association of property rights with personal liberty. Individuals needed security against both arbitrary punishment and deprivation of property. Like all of the Bill of Rights, however, these safeguards for property were binding only on the federal government.

The Fifth Amendment explicitly incorporated into the Constitution the Lockean conception that protection of property is a chief aim of government. A direct descendant of Magna Carta and the initial state constitutions, the due process clause in time became the most significant constitutional guarantee of property rights. The intended scope of the due process clause had been the subject of intense historical inquiry. It requires that judicial proceedings follow established modes of procedure. Thus, one cannot be deprived of property except by following the law of the land. But some judges and commentators early argued that the due process clause went beyond procedural regularity and also imposed a substantive limitation on the operations of government. A merely procedural safeguard would not afford much protection to property owners against legislative interference. Further, many chapters of Magna Carta are concerned with property rights and economic liberty. It thus was natural for judges steeped in the Lockean common law tradition to view due process as a substantive check against the arbitrary and unreasonable exercise of government power. The takings clause established an additional safeguard for property owners. This provision significantly limits the power of eminent domain under which government can seize private property for a public purpose. The Constitution makes no direct reference to eminent domain, but such authority is considered inherent in government as an aspect of sovereignty. Under the takings clause a person's propery cannot be seized without payment of just compensation. By giving constitutional status to the common law requirement of compensation Madison rejected outright confiscation as an acceptable policy for the federal government. Although no state convention requested a just compensation provision as part of the Bill of Rights, Madison drew on the language of the Northwest Ordinance and the Massachusetts and Vermont constitutions. The rationale behind the takings clause is that the financial burden of public policy should not be unfairly placed on individual property owners but should be shared by the public as a whole. The compensation requirement also secures property ownership by imposing a practical cost limitation on the amount of private property that the federal government can seize for public purpose.

Ratification of the Bill of Rights was completed in November 1791, two years after its submission to the states. Although the Anti-Federalists were disappointed that the proposed amendments did not afford more protection to the states, there is no evidence of opposition to either the due process or the takings clause of the Fifth Amendment. Reflecting a broad consensus on the centrality of private property in American life, these guarantees of property rights were not troubling to any segment of society.

Shortly after ratification of the Bill of Rights, Madison amplified his thinking about property rights in a brief essay that suggests a broad reading of the Fifth Amendment.[22] In language that anticipates substantive due process review of economic legislation, he observed that property was not secure "where arbitrary restrictions, exemptions, and monopolies deny to part of [the] citizens that free use of their faculties, and free choice of their occupations, which not only constitute their property in the general sense of the word; but are the means of acquiring property." Madison also decried unequal and confiscatory taxation as a

violation of property. Accordingly, he criticized a government under which "arbitrary taxes invade the domestic sanctuaries of the rich, and excessive taxes grind the faces of the poor."
    In addition, Madison addressed the question of taking private property for public use. Stressing "the inviolability of property," he noted that property could not be *"directly"* taken without compensation. Madison further declared that a government "which *indirectly* violates their property, in their actual possessions . . . is not a pattern for the United States." Because the value of property can be diminished by governmental action short of actual seizure, Madison's reference to indirect infringement indicates a generous understanding of the takings clause to encompass more than just the physical takings of property.
    A political realist, Madison was well aware that the "paper barriers" of the Bill of Rights would not necessarily secure individual liberty against the majority under all circumstances. He hoped, however, that the enumeration of fundamental rights would serve an educational function. Such restraints on the federal government, Madison reasoned, would tend "to establish the public opinion in their favor, and arouse the attention of the whole community." Even more important, Madison expected that the Bill of Rights would facilitate judicial review of actions by the federal government. "Independent tribunals of justice," Madison explained to Congress, "will consider themselves in a peculiar manner the guardians of those rights . . . they will be naturally led to resist every encroachment upon rights expressly stipulated for in the Constitution by the declaration of rights."[23] Madison proved to be a good prophet. By manifesting a national dedication to property rights, the Fifth Amendment strengthened respect for property ownership and guided subsequent constitutional development by the states and the federal courts.
    Granting explicit constitutional protection of property at the national level encouraged similar moves by the states. The federal Constitution and Bill of Rights became influential models for subsequent state constitutions. Many states borrowed the clauses designed to safeguard property ownership. When Pennsylvania revised its fundamental law in 1790, the new document added a takings and a contract clause. The South Carolina Constitution of the same year contained both a due process and a contract clause. The newer states also followed suit. For instance, the Kentucky Constitution of 1792, the Tennessee Constitution of 1796, the

Mississippi Constitution of 1817, and the Illinois Constitution of 1818 each included a contract clause, protected individuals against deprivation of property without due process, and imposed a just compensation requirement when property was taken by the state. In addition, both the Ohio Constitution of 1802 and the Illinois document placed the acquisition and possession of property among the natural rights of all persons.

These state constitutional developments were significant in two respects. First, they reinforced the high standing of property and contractual rights in the constitutional culture. Even in those states whose constitutions did not extend specific guarantees to property, the courts tended to regard such language in other documents as simply expressing fundamental tenets of American constitutionalism. Second, until the twentieth century the state governments took the lead in promoting and regulating economic activity. Yet only the federal contract clause, and later the due process clause of the Fourteenth Amendment, restricted state interference with property rights and provided a basis for federal judicial supervision of state legislation. Accordingly, the state constitutions represented an important safeguard for property owners.

Leading Federalists lost little time in utilizing the Constitution as a safeguard for property. As early as November 1788, only months after ratification was completed, several South Carolinians protested against a state law regulating the payment of debts. They asserted that the legislation violated the contract clause. By 1795 Alexander Hamilton was urging a broad understanding of the contract clause. He asserted that a state grant was the equivalent of a contract and that under the contract clause a state was constitutionally barred from breaching agreements. Thus Georgia, in Hamilton's opinion, could not revoke a land grant even if the original action were tainted by fraud.[24] Defending the controversial Jay Treaty later that year, Hamilton declared: "No powers of language at my command can express the abhorrence I feel at the idea of violating the property of individuals."[25] He went on to contend that the spirit of the contract clause should bind the federal government as well as the states and that confiscation of private debts even during wartime was contrary to the Constitution. Particularly anxious to secure credit and investment capital, the Federalists early sought to shape an intellectual climate receptive to the defense of property rights under the Constitution.

Protection of property and enhancement of commerce were at the heart of the constitution-building process. To achieve these objectives, the framers fashioned an instrument of government that limited state authority over property and trade. They further crafted institutional arrangements in order to curtail the power of the political majority to infringe on the rights of the property-owning minority. Not content to rely solely on this basic design, however, the framers also inserted many specific provisions in the Constitution and the Bill of Rights to safeguard economic rights. Utilizing the contract and due process clauses, the federal judiciary in time became a conservative bulwark of economic liberty against legislative attempts to regulate the use of property and to redistribute wealth.

The framers could look back on their handiwork with considerable satisfaction. They had checked the abuses of the revolutionary era, placed the new federal government on a firm footing, and incorporated the Lockean view of property rights into the Constitution. There remained the practical problem of translating the new scheme of government into a functioning constitutional system. A frequent problem was the need to accommodate the demands of economic growth and social change with the security of settled property rights.

4

The Development of
Property Rights
in the
Antebellum Era, 1791–1861

With the adoption of the federal Constitution, Americans turned much of their attention to encouraging economic development. There was a wide consensus in support of this objective, but sharp differences appeared over appropriate methods of realizing it.

Except as restrained by the Constitution, the state governments retained their full legislative authority. Not surprisingly, the states took the initiative in fashioning policies to stimulate economic growth. Perhaps the foremost economic problem facing the new republic was a shortage of investment capital. To overcome this deficiency the states adopted mercantilist policies. Lawmakers disposed of public land, sponsored internal improvement projects, experimented with the use of eminent domain, aided the emergence of the business corporation, granted subsidies, and modified debtor–creditor relations. These efforts toward economic development had important implications for property rights. Promotional legislation often altered existing property relationships in order to make room for new technologies and business activities. On the other hand, regulatory laws were designed to limit the use of private property or to control the conduct of business.

Indeed, state governments were the primary source of economic regulation throughout the nineteenth century. The authority of the states to regulate the use of property was derived from both common law principles and the police power. The common law doctrines of public necessity and nuisance both subordinated the rights of property owners to the interests of the general community. Under the public necessity doctrine, for instance, it was lawful to destroy buildings in order to prevent the spread of fire or pestilence.

The law of nuisance had a greater potential for limiting land usage. Even an otherwise lawful use of one's own land that unreasonably impaired the health and comfort of the general public could be deemed a public nuisance and was liable to abatement by means of an injunction. American courts in the nineteenth century modified the strict English rule of nuisance to accommodate the needs of a developing society, but landowners still faced potential liability for acts that inflicted injury on the community. Much of the nuisance litigation was directed at emerging industrial activity that caused offensive odors or excessive noise. Such obnoxious trades as pigsties and glue factories were treated as per se nuisances; that is, the very existence of these activities was deemed offensive. Noise caused by rock quarrying or smoke from a flour mill that harmed adjacent landowners could also constitute a nuisance under particular circumstances. State power to abate public nuisances provided a basis on which legislatures proscribed objectionable practices. Thus, an 1830 statute made it unlawful to store a large quantity of gunpowder in New York City. Likewise, lawmakers prohibited keeping swine in urban areas and mandated the licensing of dogs.

A more potent source of regulatory authority was the general legislative power retained by the states. The bounds of such legislative capacity was described by the awkward term *police power*. The scope of the police power proved incapable of precise delineation, but it traditionally included the authority to protect public safety, health, and morals by appropriate laws. State legislatures relied on the police power as a basis for regulating economic activity in their jurisdiction, restrained only by congressional control of interstate commerce and the property clauses of the Constitution. The exercise of state police power frequently raised constitutional issues. Although the police power was broad, the states were not free to infringe on constitutionally protected property rights or to enact legislation that conflicted with interstate commerce. Accordingly, the extent of the police power was a sensitive and recurring issue during the antebellum era.

Virtually every regulation of property limited the rights of the owner to some degree, but few questioned the authority of state governments to regulate the use and enjoyment of private property. Antebellum jurists agreed that the interests of the community prevailed over the claims of unfettered private dominion. Chief Justice Lemuel Shaw of Massachusetts explained in 1851:

> All property in this commonwealth . . . is . . . held subject to those general regulations which are necessary to the common good and general welfare. Rights of property, like all other social and conventional rights, are subject to such reasonable limitations in their enjoyment as shall prevent them from being injurious, and to such reasonable restraints and regulations established by law as the legislature, under the governing and controlling power vested in them by the constitution, may think necessary and expedient.[1]

Under the police power, state officials enjoyed broad authority to prevent an individual from using property in a manner detrimental to public order or safety. The courts sustained a variety of restrictions on the use of property as police power regulations. Among them were requirements that owners of urban lots construct buildings with inflammable materials, regulations of privately owned wharves in harbors, measures prohibiting the sale of liquor without a license, and statutes requiring railroads to institute safety features such as cattle guards. Similarly, cities could halt burials in church graveyards in order to eliminate the health hazards associated with overcrowded interment.

Slave property was also increasingly regulated in the years before the Civil War. Slaves were a form of personal property and represented a major source of wealth in the antebellum South. Owners were not legally at liberty to treat their slaves as they saw fit. Southern lawmakers recognized that slaves were human beings and enacted legislation that outlawed the killing or maiming of slaves by their master. Fearing the growth of a free black population, states passed statutes restricting the right of masters to free their slaves. Such laws deprived the owners of the right to dispose of their slave property. Moreover, slave patrols were authorized by law to enter plantations without the owner's permission and summarily punish slaves for any breaches of discipline. A large amount of community control was thus imposed on slave owners. Behind these measures was the common theme that slave property was unique and must be regulated to protect public safety.

Business activities were also a matter of concern. Persons in certain occupations, such as peddlers and auctioneers, were required to obtain licenses and comply with regulations to protect the public. Moreover, export regulations were imposed. Anxious to maintain the reputation of their crops abroad, states retained colonial schemes to control the quality of export commodities. South Carolina, for example, enacted a series of laws that provided that all tobacco be inspected in a public warehouse before being exported and that such tobacco be classified according to quality. Likewise, many localities continued the colonial practice of licensing bakers and regulating the weight and price of bread. Rejecting an argument that an assize of bread ordinance interfered with the right to pursue a lawful trade, the Supreme Court of Alabama stressed in 1841 that "the mode or manner of enjoying property" could be regulated to serve "the public interest."[2]

To modern eyes most of these economic regulations appear modest. Far from comprehensive, they were typically piecemeal and directed against specific problems. Although many of these controls did impose costs on businesses or property owners, their objective was to safeguard the general public interest. Antebellum regulations were not generally designed to transfer wealth from one portion of the population to another, and thus they produced little redistributive effect. Additionally, regulatory bodies were feeble, and enforcement often lax. Limitations on economic activities were an accepted feature of antebellum life, but narrow police power regulations allowed owners and entrepreneurs wide latitude in using their property.

State governments, moreover, were restrained by the constitutional provisions protecting private property and interstate commerce. From the outset of the new republic, the federal courts clearly signaled their intention to safeguard existing economic arrangements and to curtail state legislative authority dealing with property rights. Only three years after the ratification of the Constitution, a federal circuit court found a state debtor-relief measure to be invalid under the contract clause. In *Champion v. Casey* (1792), one of the first exercises of federal judicial review, the court held that a Rhode Island statute granting an individual debtor exemption from attachments for a period of time was an unconstitutional impairment of contract.

Looking to the precepts of natural law rather than any specific clause of the Constitution, some federal judges adopted the doctrine of vested rights to protect established property rights from legislative interference. According to the doctrine of vested rights, property ownership was a fundamental right. Laws that disturbed such rights were void because they violated the general principles limiting all constitutional governments. Justice William Paterson articulated this view in the significant circuit court case of *Vanhorne's Lessee v. Dorrance* (1795). Observing that "the right of acquiring and possessing property, and having it protected, is one of the natural, inherent and inalienable rights of man," Paterson added: "The preservation of property . . . is a primary object of the social compact."[3] After examining property ownership in terms of natural law, he implicitly linked the doctrine of natural rights with the contract clause. In a decision that anticipated the jurisprudence of John Marshall, Paterson ruled that the repeal of a Pennsylvania statute confirming certain land titles impaired the obligation of contract.

Writing a separate opinion in *Calder v. Bull* (1798) Justice Samuel Chase reiterated the vested rights doctrine. "There are certain vital principles in our free republican governments," he stated, "which will determine and overrule an apparent and flagrant abuse of legislative power." More particularly, Chase maintained that the legislature could not "violate the right of an antecedent lawful private contract; or the right of private property."[4]

John Marshall became chief justice in 1801 and dominated the Supreme Court for three decades. As a Federalist, Marshall was sympathetic to property interests and business enterprises. He distrusted state interference with economic relationships. To Marshall, property ownership both preserved individual liberty and encouraged the productive use of resources. Security of private property promoted the public interest by quickening commercial activity and thereby increasing national wealth. Consequently, Marshall sought to strengthen the bonds of the federal union, encourage the formation of a national market, and safeguard property rights from state interference. The contract clause, little debated at the constitutional convention, emerged as the centerpiece of Marshall Court jurisprudence. Drawing on the doctrine of vested rights, Marshall fashioned the contract clause into a powerful bulwark to property interests. In the words of one scholar, Marshall made the contract clause a "link between capitalism and constitutionalism."[5]

The importance of the contract clause is best understood against the background of emerging contract law. Americans in the nineteenth century shared confidence in the private ordering of the economy. The extensive use of contracts and reliance on the free market to allocate resources led J. Willard Hurst to describe this era as "above all else, the years of contract in our law."[6] Judicial insistence on the sanctity of contract, then, matched the spirit of the age by securing private arrangements from state intervention.

Marshall's initial step was to broaden the definition of contracts that were entitled to protection under the Constitution. Although the evidence is far from conclusive, it is arguable that the framers expected the clause to apply solely to state interference with private contracts. In the landmark case of *Fletcher v. Peck* (1810), however, Marshall held that a state was constitutionally barred from breaching its contracts. At issue was the huge Yazoo land grant made by the Georgia legislature in 1795 to private land companies. Amid allegations of bribery in the sale, a newly elected legislature rescinded the grant a year later. After prolonged controversy and litigation, the matter came before the Supreme Court. Marshall questioned the validity of the repeal measure on the grounds it interfered with fundamental private rights. He also noted that the terms of the contract clause "are general, and are applicable to contracts of every description." Reasoning that the repeal violated both the contract clause and "the general principles, which are common to our free institutions," Marshall declared the measure to be unconstitutional.[7] As a result of the decision in *Fletcher,* the contract clause served in the antebellum era as the most significant constitutional limitation on state power to regulate the economy.

Subsequent Supreme Court decisions broadly applied the contract clause to a variety of state economic arrangements. In *New Jersey v. Wilson* (1812) Marshall, speaking for the Court, determined that a tax exemption granted by New Jersey on a parcel of land conveyed to a band of Native Americans was a contractual right. When the Native Americans subsequently sold the land, the legislature attempted to tax the new owners. Although the power of taxation was an essential element of state sovereignty, Marshall concluded that repeal of the tax exemption impaired the obligation of contract. This case was important because antebellum lawmakers, in a desire to attract business to their state, often granted tax immunity to companies. Under the principles of *New Jersey v. Wilson* a subsequent legislature could not revoke such preferred treatment. A more far-reaching application of the contract clause occurred in *Dartmouth College v. Woodward* (1819), which held that a corporate charter was a constitutionally protected contract. There were few corporations in America before 1800, and most of these were municipal or charitable in nature. In the early nineteenth century the corporation gradually evolved into an advantageous form of business organization. Corporations offered centralized management and attracted investment capital from numerous individuals for the purpose of carrying out economic projects. Although owned and managed by private individuals, business corporations were created by a legislative charter. As the number and wealth of corporations grew, some Americans began to voice alarm over the concentration of economic power in private hands. In the popular mind, corporations were often loosely equated with monopolies. Public control of corporations therefore became a major concern, and the power of the state to repeal or alter the charter of incorporation suggested one avenue by which regulations might be imposed. Ironically, *Dartmouth College*, the leading Supreme Court decision dealing with the legal status of corporations, involved an educational rather than a business corporation.

The *Dartmouth College* case arose out of an attempt by the New Hampshire legislature to change the college's royal charter and place the institution under state control. By a five-to-one majority, the Supreme Court found that Dartmouth was a private rather than a public organization. More important, Marshall's opinion declared that a corporate charter was a "contract for the security and disposition of property," and hence a legislative alteration of its terms violated the contract clause.[8]

At first glance the *Dartmouth College* ruling seemed to aid corporate enterprise by erecting a constitutional barrier against legislative infringement of existing charters. Corporate investors and managers gained a measure of security, encouraging the rapid development of business corporations. Despite persistent controversy, corporations soon achieved a dominant position in the economy, spearheading economic growth during the nineteenth century and forging a national market for goods. In a concurring opinion, however, Justice Joseph Story suggested a means by which the states could undercut the impact of the decision. Story pointed out that state legislatures could reserve the right to modify corporate charters when they were issued. The exercise of such a reserved power would not constitute an impairment of contract. Accordingly, lawmakers commonly inserted a clause in corporate charters expressly reserving the authority to alter or repeal the instrument. Eventually state constitutions and general incorporation statutes provided that all acts were subject to this reserved power. As a result, the potential sweep of *Dartmouth College* was diminished, and the contract clause did not effectively prevent state regulation of corporate activity.

The contract clause was also a major force in shaping debtor–creditor relations. After ratification of the Constitution, many states continued the practice of enacting debtor-relief measures. Installment laws, for instance, allowed debtors to repay their obligations over an extended period of years. Other states granted stays of execution, permitted commodity payments, and experimented with bankruptcy legislation. Popular with farmers who were often in debt, relief legislation was controversial because it was redistributive in character, advancing the interests of debtors at the expense of creditors. Under the Constitution, Congress had the authority to establish a uniform system of bankruptcy. But Congress did not pass a bankruptcy statute until 1800, and this act was repealed just three years later. Without federal legislation, many states followed their established practice of permitting bankruptcy and other types of relief. Creditors vigorously attacked such laws, arguing that state debtor-relief measures represented an unconstitutional impairment of contract. Agreeing with this position, the Supreme Court of North Carolina in *Jones v. Crittenden* (1814) invalidated a law suspending executions of judgments.

A challenge to New York's bankruptcy act of 1811 came before the Supreme Court in *Sturges v. Crowninshield* (1819). Marshall's opinion addressed two principal issues. He first held that the states were free to enact bankruptcy laws until Congress exercised its power in this field. In regard to the second issue, Marshall concluded that New York's law was void because it relieved debtors of the obligation to pay debts contracted before the measure was passed. States could not retroactively discharge contractual obligations. The upshot of *Sturges* was a constitutional restriction on state power over debtor–creditor matters.

The states, however, were by no means prohibited from regulating the interests of debtors and creditors. In the course of the *Sturges* opinion,

Marshall differentiated between the obligation of contract and the legal remedies available to enforce the obligation. Because state legislatures possessed wide latitude over remedies in the state courts, lawmakers could modify remedies without running afoul of the contract clause. Imprisonment for debt, Marshall explained, could validly be abolished, leaving a creditor with recourse only against the debtor's property. This distinction between remedy and obligation gave the states room to limit the ability of creditors to collect debts, and figured prominently in subsequent decisions dealing with the contract clause.

Spurred by economic distress in wake of the Panic of 1819, many states, including New York, passed new bankruptcy laws covering only debts incurred *after* the date of enactment. By a narrow margin of four to three, the Supreme Court in *Ogden v. Saunders* (1827) sustained New York's revised statute. Speaking for the majority, Justice Bushrod Washington held that a law in effect when a contract was made formed part of the agreement. Consequently, the application of bankruptcy laws to posterior obligations did not impair any contract. Under the prevailing view, states could enact prospective laws affecting contracts but could not retrospectively alter existing contractual arrangements. In his only dissenting opinion on a constitutional issue, Marshall strongly insisted that the contract clause protected future as well as prior contractual arrangements.

The *Ogden* decision marked a watershed in the history of the contract clause. Without retreating from early decisions, the Court was henceforth guided by a more cautious spirit in contract clause cases. In *Providence Bank v. Billings* (1830), for instance, Marshall declared that the surrender of a state's power of taxation could not be implied from the grant of a charter incorporating a bank. Stressing that taxing authority "is essential to the existence of government," he rejected the contention that a tax on the corporation's capital stock impaired the obligation of contract. Significantly, Marshall added that the Constitution "was not intended to furnish the corrective for every abuse of power which may be committed by the state governments."[9] This ruling established the principle that grants of privileges and exemptions to corporations must be expressly set forth in the charter. Courts would be suspicious of claims of implied rights.

Reflecting his commitment to economic nationalism, Marshall labored for broad protection of contracts in order to encourage investment capital.

By any standard he achieved considerable success. Indeed, the contract clause figured in more Supreme Court decisions than any other section of the Constitution during the nineteenth century. Of course, several of Marshall's rulings aroused intense opposition. Most of the criticism, however, emanated from adherents of the states rights political philosophy who were alarmed at the alleged encroachments on state power. There was little hostility to Marshall's core belief that the federal courts should safeguard established economic rights.

The political triumph of Jacksonian Democracy brought new attitudes to the Supreme Court. Upon Marshall's death, President Andrew Jackson named Roger B. Taney as chief justice in 1836. Under Taney's leadership the Court shaped constitutional law to harmonize with the Jacksonian tenets of states rights, hostility to special privilege, and strict construction of the Constitution. Despite a shift of emphasis, however, the Court did not fundamentally depart from the constitutional principles of the Marshall era. Taney shared Marshall's economic values, especially the need to protect private property and to promote economic growth. Hence, the Supreme Court continued to apply vigorously the contract clause to curb state regulatory power. To be sure, there were differences in the judicial approaches of Taney and Marshall. Taney limited the reach of the contract clause and allowed the states greater flexibility to fashion economic policy. This was illustrated by *Charles River Bridge v. Warren Bridge* (1837), Taney's most famous opinion interpreting the scope of the contract clause.

The controversy in *Charles River Bridge* arose while the Transportation Revolution was transforming America. During the antebellum years new modes of transportation—turnpikes, canals, steamboats, railroads—rapidly appeared and competed for public favor. This transportation boom placed lawmakers in a dilemma. Clearly, the long-range public interest was best served by facilitating means of improving travel. At the same time, it seemed necessary to protect investors who would risk capital in often unsuccessful ventures. Many of the legal issues implicit in the Transportation Revolution, including the extent of corporate privilege, the impact of changing technology, and the conflict between economic competition and vested rights, were raised in the *Charles River Bridge* case.

Incorporated by the Massachusetts legislature in 1785, the Charles River Bridge Company was authorized to erect a toll bridge over the

Charles River. Before this charter expired, the lawmakers empowered another corporation, the Warren Bridge Company, to build a second bridge within a short distance of the original bridge. This charter provided that as soon as the cost of construction was paid, the Warren Bridge would become toll free. Because a toll bridge could not successfully compete with a free bridge, the Warren grant threatened to undercut the value of the original bridge. Nothing in the Charles River Bridge charter stated that the grant was exclusive, but the company argued that the original grant implied that it had the sole right to maintain a bridge for the life of the charter. According to this analysis, the second charter represented an impairment of the obligation of contract.

Writing for the Supreme Court, Taney rejected the notion of implied corporate privilege. Building on Marshall's opinion in *Providence Bank,* Taney declared that "no rights are taken from the public, or given to the corporation, beyond those which the words of the charter, by their natural and proper construction, purport to convey." He emphasized the principle that corporate grants must be strictly construed, a doctrine that affirmed legislative control over economic policy. This approach permitted the states, unless restrained by explicit language in a charter, to regulate corporations under the police power and to sponsor new projects for public benefit. Sensitive to the relationship between law and technology, Taney further asserted that recognition of implied corporate privileges would stymie economic progress. He astutely observed:

> If this court should establish the principles now contended for, what is to become of the numerous railroads established on the same line of travel with turnpike companies; and which have rendered the franchises of the turnpike corporations of no value? Let it once be understood that such charters carry with them these implied contracts, and give this unknown and undefined property in a line of traveling, and you will soon find the old turnpike corporations awakening from their sleep, and calling upon this court to put down the improvements which have taken their place. The millions of property which have been invested in railroads and canals, upon lines of travel which had been before occupied by turnpike corporations, will be put in jeopardy. We shall be thrown back to the improvements of the last century, and obliged to stand still, until the claims of the old turnpike corporations shall be satisfied, and they shall consent to permit these States to avail themselves of the lights of modern science, and to partake of the benefit of those improvements which are now adding to

the wealth and prosperity, and the convenience and comfort of every other part of the civilized world.[10]

To Taney's mind, existing property rights could sometimes be destroyed to make room for innovations and improvements.

In a strongly worded dissenting opinion, Justice Story set forth both legal and practical objections to the majority's position. The instrumental tone of Taney's opinion bothered Story. He contended that both common law and principles of justice supported the bridge company's exclusive right to receive tolls. The lawmakers should not be allowed to renege on their implied promise. Moreover, Story warned that if the value of investments could be undermined by legislative action, prudent individuals would not invest in projects. In short, he believed that investors were entitled to rely on the legislature's good faith in extending corporate charters. Both Story and Taney were proponents of capitalism and economic growth, but they differed over the appropriate model to achieve this goal. Story's insistence on protection for existing property rights was consistent with what one scholar has termed "his whole scheme of capitalism made moral and responsible through principled law."[11]

Despite Story's concerns in his *Charles River Bridge* dissent, the next decades were an era of rapid economic development and corporate expansion. No massive assault on corporate property took place. The Supreme Court regularly followed the principle of strict construction of grants and charters, refusing to enlarge corporate rights by implication. In essence, the Court struck a balance between private rights and the Jacksonian ideology of legislative control. Corporate grants were still protected from legislative attack under the *Dartmouth College* case, and the Court safeguarded privileges that were expressly spelled out in charters.

Eminent domain power constituted another limit on the scope of the contract clause. In *West River Bridge Company v. Dix* (1848) the Supreme Court held that the contract clause did not protect a corporation against the exercise of eminent domain. At issue was a Vermont charter authorizing a bridge company to maintain a toll bridge for one hundred years. Subsequently the state decided, as part of a highway program, to take the bridge upon payment of compensation. On behalf of the bridge company, Daniel Webster contended that the taking impaired the obligation of contract. Reasoning that all contracts were subject to the state's paramount power of eminent domain, the Supreme Court ruled that the taking was valid. Consequently, the states were free to use eminent domain to encourage transportation projects by displacing prior contractual arrangements.

Although the Supreme Court under Taney restricted the scope of the contract clause, the justices enforced the provision in cases involving debtor-relief laws, exemptions from taxation, and banking regulations. The Panic of 1837 caused some states to enact a new wave of stay laws and other measures to assist debtors. In the leading case of *Bronson v. Kinzie* (1843) the Court heard a challenge to two Illinois statutes that limited mortgage foreclosure sales and gave mortgagors broad rights to redeem foreclosed property. Both measures were retroactive, applying to mortgages made before the acts were passed. Writing for the Court, Taney found the Illinois statutes to be an unconstitutional abrogation of contract. Conceding that a state could change the remedy available to recover debts, Taney nonetheless emphasized that such alteration could not materially impair the rights of the creditors. Thus, a state that denied any remedy or provided only a burdensome procedure in effect destroyed the contractual obligation. In language reminiscent of Marshall, Taney extolled the virtue of the contract clause: "It was undoubtedly adopted as a part of the Constitution for a great and useful purpose. It was to maintain the integrity of contracts, and to secure their faithful execution throughout this Union."[12]

Constitutional issues concerning property and economic rights also arose under the commerce clause. The framers of the Constitution had been particularly anxious to foster a national market by eliminating state trade barriers. Reflecting this commitment to uniformity in commercial relations, Congress was authorized "to regulate Commerce with foreign nations, and among the several states, and with the Indian Tribes." Before the Civil War, Congress made almost no use of its legislative power under the commerce clause. Trade between the states increased markedly, however, and state regulatory legislation inevitably affected the movement of persons and goods across state lines. Thus a crucial question was the extent to which the states, under their police power, retained concurrent jurisdiction to regulate commerce in the absence of congressional legislation. As a result, during the antebellum years the Supreme Court focused on the negative or dormant effect of the commerce clause on state regulatory authority.

The first commerce clause case to reach the Supreme Court involved the burgeoning steamboat business. In 1808 the New York legislature granted Robert Fulton and Robert Livingston the exclusive right to run steamboats on the waters of New York. As might be expected, this monopoly aroused bitter feelings in adjacent states and produced retaliatory legislation. Such state restrictions on interstate commerce threatened the economic balkanization of the United States. Eventually Thomas Gibbons, operating under a federal license granted pursuant to the Coasting Act of 1793, established a rival steamboat line. The monopolists obtained an injunction against Gibbons in the New York state courts, and so he appealed to the Supreme Court.

Marshall's seminal opinion in *Gibbons v. Ogden* (1824) addressed several points. First, Marshall broadly defined commerce to include navigation and "every species of commercial intercourse" among the states. At the same time, he confined the reach of federal authority by stressing that the commerce clause did not comprehend commerce "which is completely internal, which is carried on between man and man in a state, or between different parts of the same state, and which does not extend to or affect other states." Second, Marshall described the powers of Congress, although restricted in scope, in sweeping terms. "The sovereignty of Congress," he wrote, "though limited to specified objects, is plenary as to those objects."[13] The exercise of congressional power was subject only to the controls inherent in the political process.

The most vexing question, however, was the power of the states to regulate commerce in the absence of federal action. Marshall ducked direct resolution of this issue. He noted favorably the argument that congressional power to regulate commerce implied exclusive authority to the exclusion of any state role. But Marshall relied on narrower grounds to invalidate the steamboat monopoly, concluding that the New York legislation was in conflict with the federal Coasting Act. In a gesture to the states rights doctrine, Marshall also pointed out that states could lawfully enact export inspection and quarantine laws that might have an indirect impact on commerce. Only Justice William Johnson, in a concurring opinion, found that congressional authority to regulate commerce was exclusive.

Unlike many of Marshall's decisions, the demolition of the steamboat monopoly was generally well received. The decision, moreover, had far-reaching economic effects. By maintaining interstate transportation free of state monopolies, Marshall paved the way for the development of a national railroad system. The distinguished historian Charles Warren later hailed *Ogden* as "the emancipation proclamation of American commerce."[14]

Interpretation of the commerce clause in the antebellum period was complicated by the explosive issue of slavery. A broad reading of federal commerce power seemingly jeopardized state control over commerce in slaves. This potential conflict was highlighted by the controversy over the Negro Seamen's Acts during the 1820s. Several southern states passed legislation requiring that free black sailors be detained in custody until their ship left port. Such acts interfered with the conduct of both interstate and foreign commerce, and the British government strongly protested when the laws were applied to its seamen. In *Elkison v. Deliesseline* (1823) Justice William Johnson, in a circuit court opinion, declared that South Carolina's act was incompatible with congressional power to regulate commerce. South Carolina authorities refused to comply with Johnson's ruling, and the Supreme Court never reviewed the constitutionality of the Negro Seamen's Acts. As this episode suggests, throughout the antebellum years the Supreme Court was under intense pressure to respect state police power. This in turn may explain some of the analytical confusion that characterized cases involving state power over interstate commerce.

Marshall's later commerce clause decisions also reflected sensitivity to balancing constitutionally protected commerce with state police power. In *Brown v. Maryland* (1827) Marshall curbed the states' authority to levy taxes on imported goods. He determined that state taxation of imports while in their original package in the importer's warehouse constituted an interference with interstate commerce. Conversely, Marshall ruled that the states' tax power could reach imported goods that had become "mixed up with the mass of property in the country."[15] Two years later, in *Willson v. Black Bird Creek Marsh Co.* (1829) Marshall sustained a Delaware law that authorized the building of a dam obstructing a navigable creek. Finding no governing federal statute, he held that the state measure could not "be considered as repugnant to the power to regulate commerce in its dormant state."[16] *Willson* seemingly marked a retreat from Marshall's earlier hints of an exclusive federal commerce power and pointed toward greater state regulatory authority.

Acccommodation between the national interest in uniformity and state concerns was the hallmark of commerce clause jurisprudence under Taney. In a series of decisions, starting with *New York v. Miln* (1837), the Supreme Court considered the relationship of state police power to federal authority over commerce. To control the influx of immigrant paupers, New York required the masters of ships to report certain information about passengers brought into the state. The law was challenged as an unconstitutional interference with federal power over foreign commerce. Rejecting this argument, Justice Philip B. Barbour upheld the measure as a police regulation designed to safeguard the general welfare of New York. He further intimated that unless Congress had acted, the states possessed a concurrent power to regulate commerce.

For more than a decade the Supreme Court continued to wrestle with the delineation between state police power and federal authority over commerce. Although the justices had difficulty in formulating a coherent position, they tended to expand state authority with respect to interstate commerce. In the *License Cases* (1847), for instance, the Court unanimously upheld the validity of state statutes taxing the sale of imported liquor. Yet the justices disagreed on the basis for their ruling. Taney and three other justices maintained that congressional power over commerce was not exclusive, and thus the states were free to regulate commerce unless such laws conflicted with federal legislation. In contrast, three justices argued that the state measures were not a regulation of commerce but simply an exercise of the state's police power to protect health and morals.

The doctrinal confusion over the commerce clause was substantially resolved in *Cooley v. Board of Wardens* (1852). Justice Benjamin Curtis, speaking for the Court, formulated an interpretation of the commerce power that prevailed for nearly a century. The *Cooley* case involved a Pennsylvania pilotage statute that governed foreign and interstate shipping in the port of Philadelphia. Declaring that the power to regulate commerce embraced a large field of subjects, Curtis explained that some activities needed "a single uniform rule" and were exclusively within the power of Congress.[17] On the other hand, some aspects of commerce were essentially local in nature, and the states retained concurrent authority to regulate them until Congress exerted its paramount power. Because the pilotage law came within the latter class, the Court affirmed its constitutionality. In short, under *Cooley,* state governments could exercise limited control over interstate commerce.

Curtis's opinion was seemingly a compromise, and his reasoning left something to be desired. It is difficult to reconcile the *Cooley* doctrine with the unitary language of the commerce clause. More perplexing, Curtis offered no criteria for deciding whether uniformity in regulation was necessary. The *Cooley* rule was not a tidy solution, but it established a workable and pragmatic formula for handling the disposition of commerce clause cases.

Although allowing the states to regulate some aspects of interstate commerce, the Supreme Court in *Pennsylvania v. Wheeling and Belmont Bridge Company* (1852) affirmed federal authority when state and federal law conflicted. New transportation technology and competition between steamboat and railroad interests furnished the backdrop for a challenge to the constitutionality of the Wheeling Suspension Bridge. The Virginia legislature permitted the Wheeling Bridge Company to construct a bridge spanning the Ohio River. But Pennsylvania charged that the bridge constituted a nuisance and obstructed interstate steamboat travel on a navigable river. Delivering the Court's opinion, Justice John McLean held that Congress had exercised its power to regulate navigation on the river, and consequently the bridge interfered with federal control of interstate commerce. The bridge company was ordered to abate the nuisance by modifying or removing the bridge. In an effort to overturn this decision, Congress promptly enacted a statute declaring the bridge to be a lawful structure. The Supreme Court accepted this as an exercise of congressional commerce power in a second case heard in 1856. Congress subsequently authorized the construction of numerous bridges over navigable waters. This process was cumbersome, but once again the law was shaped to encourage the growth of modern transportation at the expense of established interests.

Unlike the contract clause and the commerce power, the use of eminent domain to take private property did not receive much attention from the federal courts before the Civil War. The Constitution makes no direct reference to the power of eminent domain, but the Fifth Amendment requires that private property be taken only for "public use" and upon payment of "just compensation." Eighteenth-century judicial thinking about eminent domain was heavily influenced by natural law doctrine. In *Vanhorne's Lessee v. Dorrance* (1795), a circuit court case, Justice William Paterson concluded that the "despotic power" of taking private property "exists in every government" and that "government could not subsist without it.''[18] He stressed, however, that compensation must be paid to landowners and that the determination of land value was a judicial, not a legislative, function. Likewise, Justice James Iredell, writing in *Calder v. Bull* (1798), stated that "private rights must yield to public exigencies." Noting that public projects "are necessarily sometimes built upon the soil owned by individuals," he concluded that "justice is done" by paying landowners "a reasonable equivalent."[19] These opinions suggest that early federal judges saw eminent domain as essential to the operation of government and viewed the just compensation requirement as derived from natural law.

In practice, the takings clause of the Fifth Amendment did not bulk large during the antebellum era. The federal government undertook relatively few projects, and so there was only modest use of eminent domain. When the federal government acquired title to privately owned land for some public purpose, such as a roadway, lighthouse, or fortification, it was clear that payment of compensation was constitutionally required.

The most significant Supreme Court decision dealing with the takings clause in this period was *Barron v. Baltimore* (1833), a case illustrating that steps to enhance commercial growth could inflict hardship on individual property owners. The city of Baltimore sought to enlarge shippers' access by undertaking harbor improvements. As part of this scheme, the city diverted water from the plaintiff's wharf, thereby greatly reducing its value. The plaintiff claimed compensation for his loss under the Fifth Amendment. Rejecting this contention, the Court held that the Fifth Amendment, and by implication the entire Bill of Rights, restricted the federal government but did not apply to the states.

Following *Barron,* the states took the lead in fashioning the contours of eminent domain. The widely shared dream of a national market could not be realized without improved internal transportation. Accordingly, the state governments placed economic growth ahead of protecting the interests of landowners, aggressively using eminent domain power to promote transportation projects. This is not to suggest that state lawmakers totally disregarded the rights of landowners. Reflecting the influence of the Fifth Amendment, the constitutions of the newer states, such as Ohio and Tennessee, usually included a just compensation provision. Moreover, even when the state constitution did not expressly provide for payment, state courts reasoned that just compensation must be made under the principles of common law or natural justice. The practice that prevailed in some colonies, of taking unenclosed land for public roads without compensation, was rejected by state judges.

Although the cardinal principle of just compensation was well established during the antebellum years, state governments were short of funds and so sought to achieve economic growth at a minimum cost to taxpayers. The lawmakers thus curtailed the protection afforded to landowners in three important respects. First, the state courts encouraged an open-ended definition of public use by treating the exercise of eminent domain as a legislative responsibility. For their part, legislators delegated the power of eminent domain to business corporations for the purpose of making improvements to serve the public. As early as 1786, South Carolina conferred the power of eminent domain on the Santee Canal Company to obtain land and materials for the construction of a canal. Soon antebellum lawmakers were regularly extending this privilege to canal and railroad companies.

Second, state courts tended to adopt a narrow view of what actions constituted a taking of property for which compensation was required. Improvements of roads and alterations in the natural flow of watercourses, as part of schemes to enhance transportation, often depreciated the value of adjacent land. River navigation projects, for example, sometimes obstructed the flow of water necessary to operate mills. Yet courts usually regarded such injury to property as consequential damage that did not call for payment. Most antebellum judges took the position that there must be a direct appropriation of title rather than merely a diminution of value in order to receive compensation. This judicial attitude had led some historians to argue that landowners were in effect compelled to subsidize public improvements.

Third, legislators and judges attempted to limit application of the compensation principle. They adopted the practice of offsetting the imputed benefits of a project against the loss suffered by individual property owners whose land was taken. An 1835 Georgia railroad statute, for instance, required that in awarding compensation the appraisers must consider "the benefit and advantage" that a landowner received "from the erection and establishment of the railroad or works." This approach minimized the cost of employing eminent domain by effectively placing much of the burden of economic development on the landowners.

As might be expected, the large-scale use of eminent domain proved controversial. Daniel Webster, arguing before the Supreme Court in *West River Bridge Company v. Dix* (1848), attacked legislative discretion over eminent domain and urged judicial supervision by the federal courts. If "the legislature," he warned, "or their agents are to be the sole judges of what is to be taken, and to what public use it is to be appropriated, the most levelling ultraisms of Anti-rentism or agrarianism or Abolitionism may be successfully advanced."[20] Webster's plea was unheeded before the Civil War, but later in the nineteenth century the Supreme Court began to fashion the takings cause of the Fifth Amendment into a more powerful shield for property owners.

Like the takings clause, the due process clause of the Fifth Amendment did not play a large role in the constitutional safeguarding of economic interests before the Civil War. As noted earlier, the origin of the due process clause can be traced to the language "by the law of the land" in Magna Carta. In fact, this older wording appeared in many of the first state constitutions. Historically the guarantee of due process was defined largely in procedural terms, requiring simply that customary legal procedures be followed before a person could be punished for criminal offenses. Indeed, Alexander Hamilton explained in 1787 that due process was a technical concept applicable only to judicial process. The purpose of due process, then, was to protect individuals against arbitrary punishment.

By the late eighteenth century, however, state courts began to wrestle with substantive interpretations of due process. Several of these early cases arose out of legislative attempts to transfer private property from one party to another. The outcome of this litigation manifested judicial concern for the security of private ownership. Courts started gingerly to view the "law of the land" clauses in state constitutions as restricting legislative control of property. Not every legislative action necessarily satisfied the due process requirement. In 1792, for instance, the South Carolina Court of Common Pleas held that "it was against common right, as well as against *magna charta,* to take away the freehold of one man and vest it in another, and that, too, to the prejudice of third persons, without any compensation, or even a trial by the jury of the country, to determine the right in question."[21] The 1805 decision in *University of North Carolina v. Foy* was even more telling. Relying on the "law of the land" provision in North Carolina's constitution, the court invalidated the repeal of an act granting land to university trustees. Because the due process guarantee limited legislative power, lawmakers could not, by fiat, divest a person of property ownership. In *Wynehamer v. People* (1856) the New York Court of Appeals enlarged the scope of due process to protect the right to use property. At issue was a statute outlawing the sale of liquor. Finding this measure to be a deprivation of property without due process as applied to liquor owned when the law took effect, the Court observed that "the legislature cannot totally annihilate commerce in any species of property, and so condemn the property itself to extinction."[22] This significant case was the first time that a court determined that the concept of due process prevented the legislature from regulating the beneficial enjoyment of property in such a manner as to destroy its value.

This emerging doctrine of substantive due process went beyond traditional guarantees of orderly procedure and imposed restraints on legislative actions that unreasonably infringed on fundamental but un-written rights. Because property ownership had long been closely associ-ated with individual liberty, by the mid-nineteenth century judges in-creasingly invoked substantive due process to defend property rights against economic regulations. Courts broadly reviewed legislation and struck down laws deemed unreasonable as deprivations of property without due process.

Federal courts also adopted the view that due process limited legisla-tive discretion. In *Murray's Lessee v. Hoboken Land and Improvement Co.* (1856) the Supreme Court insisted that the due process clause of the Fifth Amendment was "a restraint on the legislative as well as on the executive and judicial powers of the government, and cannot be so construed as to leave congress free to make any process 'due process of law,' by its mere will."[23] Although in *Murray's Lessee* the Court was considering a procedural issue, the opinion suggested a larger measure of judicial authority that could easily provide a basis for substantive review of congressional legislation.

Substantive due process first appeared in federal jurisprudence in the controversial 1857 *Dred Scott* decision. Chief Justice Roger Taney interpreted the due process clause as placing a substantive limitation on the power of Congress with respect to slave property in the territories. The *Dred Scott* ruling was effectively superseded by the Civil War and the Fourteenth Amendment, but the concept of substantive due process was destined for a robust rebirth in a later generation. After the Civil War, both federal and state courts vigorously employed substantive due process to safeguard economic liberty from legislative control.

Patent and copyright law also raised important issues of property rights and community interests during the antebellum era. The Constitution authorized Congress to grant limited monopolies to inventors and authors for the purpose of encouraging technology and literary production. In 1790 Congress passed legislation securing both copyrights and patents. A separate Patent Office was created in 1836 to handle the growing number of patent applications. Because the nineteenth century was a period of rapid technological change, the federal courts had to reconcile claims of monopoly property rights in inventions and literary works with the republican dislike of special privilege and desire to disseminate knowledge widely. The Supreme Court's first ruling on the law of intellectual property was *Wheaton v. Peters* (1834). Concluding that there was no common law copyright, the Court held that a statutory copyright could be obtained only by strict compliance with the terms of the 1790 act. Reflecting the Jacksonian hostility to monopolies, the *Wheaton* decision established that copyright protection was designed to benefit the public and was therefore confined to the narrow limits set by Congress.

Legal scholarship reinforced the importance of property rights in antebellum jurisprudence. James Kent, an eminent New York judge, wrote the popular and influential *Commentaries on American Law* (1826–30), providing a definitive interpretation of American law. New editions appeared regularly, and Kent had an enormous impact on subsequent legal developments. Strongly supportive of property ownership, Kent classed "the right to acquire and enjoy property" among the "absolute rights of individuals."[24] In Kent's view, government was obligated to protect property owners. He stressed the requirement of compensation when private propery was taken for public use. To be sure, Kent agreed that in certain situations property rights were subservient to the public welfare. Hence, government could validly prohibit nuisances and dangers to health. But Kent believed that the security of property ownership and corporate enterprise encouraged economic growth, and consequently he emphasized the constitutional restrictions on governmental authority over property.

Antebellum legal culture placed a high value on the security of property. Despite their differences, the leading jurists of this period, Marshall, Taney, Story, and Kent, envisioned respect for property rights

broader in scope. All property of persons who favored the Confederacy was declared subject to forfeiture. In an important step toward emancipation, the act freed the slaves of Confederate sympathizers who escaped or were captured by the Union forces. Although reminiscent of the seizure of Loyalist property during the Revolution, the two Confiscation acts followed traditional procedures requiring a judicial determination of guilt in individual cases. In fact these laws were largely unenforced and had little impact. Reluctant to attack property rights, many federal officials were ambivalent about confiscation as a policy and never promoted forfeiture proceedings.

The drive to abolish the most controversial form of property—slavery—accelerated as the Civil War continued. Prepared to respect the rights of slave owners, Lincoln initially favored gradual emancipation with compensation paid by the federal government. He repeatedly urged such schemes on Congress. Indeed, in April 1862 Congress abolished slavery in the District of Columbia, with compensation to loyal owners. Anxious to increase pressure on the Confederacy, however, in September 1862 Lincoln issued a preliminary proclamation of emancipation. Based on his power as commander in chief, Lincoln declared that all slaves in the rebellious states would be freed on January 1, 1863. Lincoln constitutionally justified the subsequent Emancipation Proclamation "as a fit and necessary war measure for suppressing said rebellion."[1] Despite the symbolic importance of the Emancipation Proclamation, Lincoln's action was attacked by conservatives as unconstitutional, and it had limited practical effect, as most slaves were behind Confederate lines. Although Maryland and Missouri ended slavery during the Civil War, the legal position of slave property was still unsettled when the hostilities ended. Ratification of the Thirteenth Amendment in 1865 completed the process of abolishing slavery. The property interests of slave owners were eliminated without compensation, an instance of massive governmental interference with existing economic relationships to achieve societal goals.

The war effort also compelled the federal government to play an active role in managing the economy. The Civil War created an unprecedented demand for expenditures. Yet financing the war was a vexing task, hampered by inadequate revenue and the lack of a national banking system. Consequently, Congress experimented with new methods of public finance. In 1861 it levied the first income tax, a flat tax of 3 percent

on income over $800 a year. The rates were later increased, and this tax remained in force until 1872. In addition, the government issued large amounts of paper money not redeemable in gold or silver, popularly known as *greenbacks*. The Legal Tender Act of 1862 declared such paper-money notes to be lawful tender for all debts and the payment of taxes. But the greenback dollars rapidly depreciated in value, and creditors resisted attempts to discharge debts with such currency. Further, in 1864 Congress organized the national banking system and established a uniform currency of national banknotes. A year later Congress placed a heavy tax on state banknotes, effectively driving them out of circulation as currency.

All of these measures were controversial, but the Supreme Court sustained these fledgling moves toward national regulation of the economy. In *Springer v. United States* (1881) the Court upheld the Civil War income tax as applied to professional earnings. The justices rejected the contention that the levy constituted an unconstitutional direct tax. Also significant was the decision in *Veazie Bank v. Fenno* (1869), in which the Supreme Court affirmed the power of Congress to tax the notes of state banks. Stressing the importance of securing a uniform currency, the Court refused to scrutinize the motives of Congress in levying such a prohibitive tax. Thus, *Veazie Bank* established that Congress could use its taxing power to regulate or even eliminate particular economic activities.

Far more provocative was the Court's handling of the constitutional challenges to the legal tender legislation. In *Hepburn v. Griswold* (1870) the Supreme Court, by a vote of four to three, declared the act invalid as applied to contracts made *before* its passage. Speaking for the Court, Chief Justice Salmon P. Chase concluded that the act violated the due process clause of the Fifth Amendment and impaired the obligation of contract in a manner inconsistent with the spirit of the Constitution. An intense public debate ensued. Many in business and government feared economic chaos as a result of this ruling. On the very day the Supreme Court decided *Hepburn*, President Ulysses S. Grant nominated two new justices to fill Court vacancies. The government lost no time in requesting a reargument of the legal tender matter before the reconstituted Court. In *Knox v. Lee* (1871) the Court, by a margin of five to four, overruled *Hepburn* and upheld the constitutionality of the Legal Tender Act with respect to both *preexisting* and *subsequent* contracts. The upshot of the

Legal Tender Cases was judicial recognition of broad congressional power over the currency and monetary policy. In other areas of economic activity, however, the Supreme Court proved less deferential to legislative authority.

Following the Civil War, America experienced an era of enormous economic growth. Spearheaded by the railroads, industrial development and technological innovation proceeded rapidly. Corporate enterprises extended their operations across state lines and created a national market for goods. Rapid industrialization, however, produced economic dislocation, and not all segments of society benefited from the unbridled operation of the market economy. Plagued by low crop prices, farmers in the Middle West were often hostile to the interests of eastern investors and the business community. In the 1870s many farmers were attracted to the Granger movement, and agrarian discontent fueled demands for legislation to assist farmers. State legislatures heeded these cries for reform by enacting laws to control corporate enterprise and insulate local markets from competition. Such regulations of business increasingly entailed some redistribution of property to benefit distressed groups. In response, corporations and property owners looked to the judiciary for protection. They sought to utilize the Fourteenth Amendment as a shield against state legislation that, in their view, represented arbitrary and unreasonable interference with economic rights.

The first interpretation of the Fourteenth Amendment came in the *Slaughterhouse Cases* (1873). During Reconstruction the Louisiana legislature created a monopoly of the slaughterhouse business in New Orleans and banned other persons from engaging in that activity. By centralizing and regulating slaughterhouse operations the lawmakers hoped to eliminate health hazards to adjacent neighborhoods. Many localities enacted similar measures, justifying them as exercises of the police power. In Louisiana the monopoly privilege was conferred on a group of individuals with close political ties to the Reconstruction government. This prompted charges of political corruption.

Some New Orleans butchers challenged the Louisiana statute, arguing that the monopoly deprived them of the property right to pursue a trade in violation of both the privileges or immunities clause and the due process clause of the Fourteenth Amendment. By a five-to-four vote the Supreme Court rejected this contention and placed a narrow construction on the scope of the privileges or immunities clause. According to the Court, there was no federally protected right to be free of monopoly. The Court majority was not willing to recognize any fundamental change in the authority of the federal government over the states as a result of the Fourteenth Amendment. In sharp contrast, the dissenting justices saw the amendment as a substantive restraint on state power to regulate the rights of property owners. Attacking monopolies as an encroachment on the right to acquire property, Justice Stephen J. Field argued that the right to pursue a lawful occupation was protected by the Fourteenth Amendment. Justice Joseph P. Bradley espoused a dynamic view of property as encompassing economic opportunity. Anticipating the doctrine of economic due process, he declared that "a law which prohibits a large class of citizens from adopting a lawful employment . . . does deprive them of liberty as well as property without due process of law."[2]

The Supreme Court next considered the authority of the states to control private property in *Munn v. Illinois* (1877). Farmers directed much of their anger against railroads and related utilities, which they perceived as wielding undue economic power, and they blamed for excessive charges. During the 1870s, midwestern and southern state legislatures enacted so-called Granger laws to regulate the prices charged by railroads and grain elevators. They also established commissions to supervise railroad operations. At issue in *Munn* was an Illinois statute that set the rate for storing grain in Chicago elevators. The elevator managers assailed this measure as both a deprivation of property without due process of law and an impermissible regulation of interstate commerce by a state.

Upholding the Illinois law, the Supreme Court again adopted a deferential attitude toward state authority to control the use of private property. Speaking for the Court, Chief Justice Morrison R. Waite ruled that "when private property is devoted to a public use, it is subject to public regulation."[3] Whether this public interest doctrine applied to a particular enterprise was considered a matter for legislative judgment. Although recognizing that the owner of property "clothed with a public interest" was entitled to reasonable compensation, Waite further declared that the determination of such compensation was a legislative, not a judicial, task. The only protection of property owners against legislative abuse was resort to the political process. Lastly, Waite concluded that the Illinois law was primarily a local regulation with only an indirect impact on interstate commerce. Field vigorously dissented, warning that under the *Munn* rationale "all property and all business in the State are held at the mercy of a majority of its legislature."[4] Stating that grain storage was a private business, he maintained that the due process clause afforded substantive protection to owners in the use of and income from their property.

During the 1880s judicial attitudes began to change, and Field's views gradually gained ascendancy. The Supreme Court receded from the deferential approach of *Munn* and adopted a more skeptical posture toward state regulation of property and business. This new outlook was closely tied to emerging constitutional and economic thought. Thomas M. Cooley's influential *Treatise on the Constitutional Limitations Which Rest upon the Legislative Power of the States* (1868) was instrumental in fashioning the due process clause into a substantive restraint on state power to regulate economic rights. As suggested by the title of his treatise, Cooley's primary goal was to impose limits on arbitrary legislative action. Linking the concept of due process with the earlier doctrine of vested rights, Cooley paved the way for a broad reading of the Fourteenth Amendment. Moreover, Cooley fused the Jacksonian principles of equal rights and hostility to special economic privilege with due process protection of property rights. From this libertarian basis he sharply questioned the constitutionality of class legislation, laws that benefited one segment of society at the expense of another. In later years Cooley criticized the *Munn* opinion and argued that state control of private business threatened individual liberty.

Another significant laissez-faire theorist, Christopher G. Tiedeman, mirrored Cooley's views.[5] In his book, *A Treatise on the Limitations of Police Power in the United States* (1886), Tiedeman advanced a narrow conception of the police power. He sharply criticized most governmental intervention in the economy and urged judicial protection of free-market principles. Tiedeman maintained that the freedom to enter contracts was a property right not subject to general state regulation. Thus, he directly contributed to the evolution of the liberty of contract doctrine.

Cooley and Tiedeman gave impetus to the widespread acceptance of laissez-faire constitutionalism. Laissez-faire advocates shared a deep aversion to state-sanctioned monopoly and viewed with suspicion any government intervention into the market economy. Consistent with the Jacksonian heritage, proponents of laissez-faire constitutionalism insisted that the government could not legitimately aid one class or group against another. Attorneys for corporate enterprise were quick to urge this doctrine on the Supreme Court. They repeatedly contended that regulatory statutes exceeded legislative authority and particularly attacked laws seeking to redress hardships by redistributing wealth.[6]

The fundamental concerns of laissez-faire proponents, however, went beyond the entrenchment of economic privilege. They saw a close connection between economic liberty and the protection of personal freedom against governmental authority.[7] Harking back to the tenets of Jacksonian Democracy, laissez-faire spokesmen genuinely feared that demands for special-interest or class legislation would undermine liberty and democratic government. Prominent laissez-faire adherents therefore opposed protective tariffs, subsidies, and other legislation that benefited business. The judicial philosophy of Justice John M. Harlan illustrates the link between laissez-faire philosophy and liberty. To Harlan the freedom to own and use property was an important element of personal liberty. He was instrumental in fashioning the doctrines of economic due process and liberty of contract, both mainstays of laissez-faire constitutionalism. Yet Harlan also championed the rights of racial minorities and criminal defendants.

Because judges are influenced by social forces and intellectual currents in general society, the principles of laissez-faire constitutionalism gained currency among Supreme Court justices in the 1880s. They began to formulate doctrines that curtailed the exercise of state police power and enlarged the scope of economic liberty. In *Stone v. Farmers' Loan & Trust Co.* (1886) the Court upheld a Mississippi statute that empowered a commission to regulate railroad rates but cautioned that such authority was not unlimited. Chief Justice Waite added that ''the State cannot require a railroad corporation to carry persons or property without reward; neither can it do that which in law amounts to a taking of private property for public use without just compensation, or without due process of law.''[8] The Court ruled in another case that corporations were persons within the meaning of the Fourteenth Amendment and thus were entitled to protection under the due process clause.

In *Mugler v. Kansas* (1887) the Supreme Court went a step further, moving toward a substantive interpretation of the due process clause to safeguard fundamental property rights.[9] This step laid the foundation for the doctrine of economic due process. A brewer challenged the constitutionality of a Kansas prohibition law as a deprivation of property without due process. Although the Court sustained the prohibition measure as a valid use of the state police power to protect health and morals, Justice Harlan emphasized that courts could scrutinize the purpose behind state regulation as well as the means employed to achieve the stated ends. The Court, Harlan cautioned, need not accept a legislative exercise of the police power at face value. Rather, he declared that courts were under a duty to "look at the substance of things" and determine whether the provisions of the statute bore any real relationship to its ostensible purpose. Moreover, Harlan insisted that there were "limits beyond which legislation cannot rightfully go."[10] Under *Mugler,* laws that purported to protect health, safety, or morals might in fact unreasonably deprive an owner of property without due process. The effect of this decision was to assert far-reaching federal judicial supervision of state economic legislation.

Significantly, during the 1880s several state supreme courts also interpreted due process as protecting economic rights against legislative controls. In 1885, for instance, the New York Court of Appeals invalidated a statute restricting the manufacture of cigars in tenements. Denying that the law had any relation to public health, the Court reasoned that it arbitrarily deprived the tenement owner and the tenants of both property and personal liberty. Courts in Pennsylvania and Illinois similarly relied on due process as a basis to review legislative controls on business.

Economic due process soon became the most important judicial instrument safeguarding property rights and vindicating the principles of laissez-faire constitutionalism. The Supreme Court early applied economic due process in the field of railroad regulation: State imposed rates had made it difficult for many interstate railroads to operate profitably. Anxious to defend investment capital against impairment by unduly low rates, the Supreme Court took particular aim at state laws regulating railroads and utilities. In a series of decisions during the 1890s, the Court ruled that utilities were constitutionally entitled to charge reasonable rates and that the determination of reasonableness was a judicial question. This movement culminated in *Smyth v. Ames* (1898), in which the Court unanimously held that a utility must be allowed a "fair return upon the value of that which it employs for public convenience."[11] The *Smyth* formula required that rates be based on a company's present value and promulgated a complex test to ascertain such value. The outcome was to greatly restrict state rate-making authority over railroads and utilities. This increasing judicial supervision of rate regulation reflected concern that the states fixed inadequate rates and thereby discouraged necessary investments in large-scale projects. Accordingly, the Court fashioned constitutional guarantees for utilities and effectively abandoned the permissive *Munn* doctrine.

The Supreme Court also developed an important corollary of economic due process, the liberty of contract doctrine. In *Allgeyer v. Louisiana* (1897) the Court invalidated a state law that prohibited a person from obtaining insurance from a company that was not qualified to do business in Louisiana. The Court reasoned that liberty, as protected by the Fourteenth Amendment, encompassed the right to "enter into all contracts which may be proper" to pursue an occupation or acquire property.[12] States could not interfere with this contractual freedom, a position that cast a deep shadow over legislative attempts to regulate the terms of employment. Incorporating laissez-faire values, the liberty of contract doctrine proceeded on the assumption that both parties to a contract enjoyed relatively equal bargaining power and should be allowed to determine freely contractual terms. Liberty of contract preserved private decision making in economic matters and safeguarded the market value of property and services.

Because numerous state regulations placed some degree of restriction on property ownership or contractual obligations, the implications of economic due process were potentially sweeping. In essence, the Supreme Court assessed economic regulations against a reasonableness standard and struck down measures deemed unduly restrictive of property rights or serving the interests of only one class. As the Court explained in *Lawton v. Steele* (1894): "The legislature may not, under the guise of protecting the public interests, arbitrarily interfere with private business, or impose unusual and unnecessary restrictions upon lawful occupations."[13]

Although laissez-faire constitutionalism became predominant during the 1890s, the Court also recognized that states could lawfully restrict property and contractual rights in appropriate situations under the police power. Consequently, the scope of the police power was a crucial issue. The justices were usually sympathetic to laws protecting the health, safety, and morals of society. In *Holden v. Hardy* (1898), for instance, by a vote of seven to two the Supreme Court upheld a Utah statute that limited the period of employment in mines to eight hours a day. Rejecting a challenge based on the liberty of contract doctrine, the Court stressed the unhealthy conditions of mine work and realistically noted that mine owners and their employees ''do not stand upon an equality, and that their interests are, to a certain extent, conflicting.''[14] The justices also upheld state legislation that abolished the fellow servant rule for railroads, thus enlarging the employer's tort liability to employees injured at work. Moreover, the Court ruled that states could regulate the taking of fish and game and could summarily destroy illegal nets. On balance, the Supreme Court actually overturned few regulatory measures. Still, under economic due process the Court established its right to review the reasonableness of statutes and required state governments to justify their interference with property rights.

In addition to fashioning the doctrine of economic due process, the Supreme Court enlarged the protection available to property owners under the takings clause of the Fifth Amendment. As the country became more settled and prosperous, the value of land increased. Accordingly, the justices constrained the use of eminent domain power in several respects. The Court broadened the definition of a taking in *Pumpelly v. Green Bay Company* (1871), holding that a physical invasion that destroyed the usefulness of land was a taking, even though title technically remained in the owner. For example, when land was permanently flooded by overflow from a dam, the owner was constitutionally entitled to compensation.

Further, the Supreme Court gave an expansive reading to the just compensation requirement in *Monongahela Navigation Company v. United States* (1893). Observing that the compensation principle ''prevents the public from loading upon one individual more than his just share of the burdens of government,'' the Court reiterated that the assessment of an indemnity payment was a judicial, not a legislative, task. Speaking for the Court, Justice David J. Brewer ruled that the owner must receive ''a full and exact equivalent'' and that the value of property was determined by its profitableness.[15] Even more important, in *Chicago, Burlington and Quincy Railroad Company v. Chicago* (1897) the justices unanimously held that the just compensation requirement constituted an essential element of due process as guaranteed by the Fourteenth Amendment. Accordingly, the just compensation rule became in effect the first provision of the Bill of Rights to be applied to the states.

At the same time, the Court was cool toward the claim that regulations limiting the use of property represented an unconstitutional taking without compensation. A Kansas law, for instance, prohibited the manufacture or sale of liquor and ordered the destruction of liquor already in stock. By preventing the use of breweries for their intended purpose, the statute drastically reduced the value of land and equipment to the owners. Stressing that this legislation did not disturb the owners' use of property for lawful activities, the Court in *Mugler v. Kansas* (1887) stated that a "prohibition simply upon the use of property for purposes that are declared by valid legislation, to be injurious to the health, morals, or safety of the community, cannot, in any sense, be deemed a taking or an appropriation of property for the public benefit."[16] In a dissenting opinion, however, Justice Field refused to concede that the legislature could limit the use of land without compensation and found that the destruction of liquor and brewing utensils "crossed the line which separates regulation from confiscation."[17]

The contract clause continued to figure in constitutional policy after the Civil War. Indeed, the Supreme Court expanded the reach of the contract clause to encompass arrangements made in reliance on judicial interpretation of state law. The city of Dubuque issued bonds to aid railroad construction following an Iowa Supreme Court decision that such bonds were lawful under the state constitution. The railroad failed, however, to generate the anticipated revenue, and the city found it difficult to pay interest on the bonds. Thereafter the Iowa court reversed its position and declared the bonds invalid. In a suit by bondholders, the United States Supreme Court in *Gelpcke v. City of Dubuque* (1864) sustained the validity of the bond issue as a contract that could not be impaired by a changed interpretation of state law. The justices seemingly ruled that the contract clause protected the legitimate expectation of the parties from subsequent judicial as well as legislative interference. Reflecting a deep distrust of public debt repudiation, the *Gelpcke* decision provided a judicial check on municipal bond policies. In the 1870s the Court applied the *Gelpcke* rule in a series of cases and upheld the issuance of municipal bonds worth millions of dollars. The upshot was judicial protection of investment capital against repudiation by local governments, a move consistent with the policy of stimulating economic growth.

Nonetheless, during the late nineteenth century the contract clause was gradually eclipsed by economic due process as the primary constitutional safeguard of property and business interests. Several factors explain the declining importance of the contract clause. By its terms the contract clause applied solely to the states and afforded no protection from federal regulation. Moreover, it was well settled that the clause prohibited only laws that retrospectively impaired existing contracts. States were free to enact prospective legislation governing future contractual arrangements. Although under *Dartmouth College* corporate charters were still treated as protected contracts, state legislatures undercut this rule by reserving the power to repeal or amend charters, substantially without limit. The Supreme Court generally sustained these reservation clauses, permitting the alteration of chartered rights. Consequently, the broad and flexible doctrine of economic due process, with its reasonableness standard, proved more attractive to proponents of laissez-faire constitutionalism. Propertied interests increasingly looked to the due process clause to defend economic rights.

The Supreme Court contributed to this result by rendering decisions that diluted the protection of the contract clause. First, in a series of rate regulation cases during the 1880s, the Court insisted that corporate charters be strictly construed. Corporations claiming exemption from legislative control were required to demonstrate clearly this privilege by express language in their charter. Even when charters seemingly granted railroads the power to set their own rates, the Court was disinclined to apply the contract clause to state regulation. As a consequence of this restrictive view, railroads and utilities received little solace from the contract clause. Indeed, after 1890 most rate regulation cases were handled under the due process clause, not the contract clause.

Of greater significance, in *Fertilizing Company v. Hyde Park* (1878), the justices recognized a police power exception to the contract clause. A corporation had statutory authorization to operate a fertilizer plant in a particular location for fifty years, but subsequently a municipal ordinance prohibited the transportation of offal through the streets. Although this action halted the operation of the factory, the Supreme Court rejected the company's position that the ordinance violated the contract clause. Instead, the Court pointed out that contractual arrangements were subject to the state's power to abate a nuisance. Two years later the Court explicitly established that a state legislature could not bargain away its essential authority over public health and morals. All contracts were subject to the police power. Thus, in *Stone v. Mississippi* (1880) the

Court held that a state could forbid the sale of lottery tickets, even though a previous charter had granted the right to operate lotteries. This concept of inalienable police power opened the door for state legislatures to interfere with contracts in order to protect the public.

Closely related to the police power exception was the public trust doctrine. At issue in *Illinois Central Railroad v. Illinois* (1892) was an 1869 statute granting a large area of submerged land along the Chicago waterfront to the railroad. The legislature later repealed this law and sought to reclaim the land. Brushing aside the argument that Illinois was impairing its contract, the Court held, by a narrow four-to-three margin, that a state could not irrevocably alienate land under navigable waters. Speaking for the Court, Justice Field reasoned that such lands were held in trust for the public and could be granted only to the limited extent that their disposition was consistent with the public interest in navigation and commerce. Because any transfer of public trust land was necessarily revocable, no contractual obligation was impaired. Invocation of the open-ended public trust doctrine further diminished the protection of the contract clause.

Moreover, faced with widespread repudiation of bonds by the southern states, the Supreme Court evaded application of the contract clause on jurisdictional grounds. Following Reconstruction many southern states sought to escape payment of their large bonded indebtedness. With vast sums at stake, investors flocked to the federal courts, alleging that the refusal of states to honor their bonds transgressed the contract clause. Unwilling to rekindle sectional controversy, the Court in a series of cases ruled that private suits in federal court to compel states to perform their obligations were forbidden by the Eleventh Amendment.[18] In effect the justices refused to enforce the payment of state debts and thereby permitted a violation of the contract clause. Because of an unusual feature of Virginia bonds, however, the Court in the *Virginia Coupon Cases* (1885) found that the Old Dominion had breached the contract clause and must honor its bonds.

In contrast with its handling of state bond repudiation, the Supreme Court applied the contract clause to counties and municipalities, forcing local governments to pay their obligations. The justices determined that local governments could not claim shelter from lawsuits in federal court under the Eleventh Amendment. Political circumstances explain the different judicial treatment of states and localities. Because most defaulting cities and counties were in the western states, the Supreme Court could coerce payment of bonded debt without reopening sectional wounds. The Court heard hundreds of municipal bond cases during the Gilded Age, and judicial insistence on fiscal probity strengthened the credit rating of cities and counties.

Notwithstanding these decisions regarding municipal bonds, the contract clause played only a secondary role in the protection of economic interests during the Gilded Age. The Supreme Court heard many cases challenging state laws on contract clause grounds, but state actions were rarely invalidated on this basis. Certainly the contract clause no longer assumed the same importance as it had in the antebellum era. Ironically the Supreme Court enunciated the novel liberty of contract doctrine while often ignoring the express constitutional provision prohibiting state impairment of existing contracts.

Another provision of the Constitution also had a significant impact on contractual relationships. The bankruptcy clause effectively empowers Congress to impair contracts and override private economic arrangements. Bankruptcy is a process by which a court takes control of a debtor's property, distributes it among creditors, and discharges the debtor from future liability for existing obligations. The exercise of the bankruptcy power remained a controversial subject in the Gilded Age. Early in the nineteenth century Congress passed several short-lived bankruptcy laws. Repeal of these measures left control over debtor–creditor relations in state hands. With the growth of interstate business, commercial enterprises favored uniform trade laws and urged a national bankruptcy system. Farmers and debtors, on the other hand, were suspicious of federal bankruptcy legislation, preferring to rely on state laws for debt relief. Opinion also divided along sectional lines. Anxious to defend local interests against northern creditors, southerners were particularly opposed to the imposition of national bankruptcy standards. The Panic of 1893, however, demonstrated the need for federal bankruptcy legislation.

After years of acrimonious debate, Congress in 1898 finally enacted an enduring bankruptcy measure. The act took account of the competing concerns of debtors and creditors. Debtors, except corporations, could voluntarily claim the benefits of bankruptcy to obtain a discharge from pressing obligations and thus gain a fresh start. Creditors could involuntarily force insolvent debtors into bankruptcy as a means of securing payment of debts and equitable distribution of assets. However, farmers and wage earners could not be forced into bankruptcy. In time, the national bankruptcy system gained general acceptance, and the basic principles of the 1898 act, with modifications, have continued to the present.

The Supreme Court also wrestled with the commerce clause in light of the new industrial order and the emerging national market. During the late nineteenth century the states remained the primary locus of regulatory authority. Yet attempts by the states to cope with economic forces threatened to obstruct interstate commerce. Before the Civil War the Court had interpreted the commerce clause to restrict implicitly the states' power to regulate interstate business. There was, however, considerable uncertainty with respect to both the scope of the commerce clause and which state regulations impermissibly interfered with interstate commerce.

Occasionally there was a conflict between federal and state regulation of business enterprise. In *Pensacola Telegraph Company v. Western Union Telegraph Company* (1877) Western Union was operating under a congressional grant to maintain telegraph lines anywhere in the United States. Florida gave Pensacola Telegraph an exclusive privilege to conduct such a business in certain counties. Holding that telegraph communications constituted interstate commerce, the Court broadly stated that the congressional powers over commerce "keep pace with the progress of the country, and adapt themselves to the new developments of time and circumstances."[19] Because the Florida franchise contradicted the federal act, the justices sustained Western Union's position.

For the most part there was no federal legislation governing business activities, and the Supreme Court had difficulty formulating a standard by which to determine the extent of allowable state regulation of interstate commerce. As so often in the Gilded Age, the railroads were at the center of the problem. By the 1880s, state regulation of interstate railroad operations had proved inadequate from every perspective. The states could not meaningfully control long-distance transportation, and the railroads faced a chaotic assortment of inconsistent state regulations and rates. Taking another step away from *Munn*, the Supreme Court held in *Wabash, St. Louis & Pacific Railway v. Illinois* (1886) that state regulation of interstate rates invaded federal power under the commerce clause. The Court reasoned that "this species of regulation is one which must be, if established at all, of a general and national character, and cannot be safely and wisely remitted to local rules and local regulations."[20]

In response, Congress passed the Interstate Commerce Act (1887), the first major affirmative exercise of federal regulatory authority under the commerce clause. The act declared that charges for interstate railroad transportation should be reasonable and just, but it did not define such a rate. Further, the act outlawed rate-fixing arrangements, rebates to preferred shippers, and rate discrimination against short-haul shippers. Using the model of existing state regulations, the act also created a new agency, the Interstate Commerce Commission (ICC), with the power to conduct hearings and issue orders to halt practices violating the statute. Influenced by laissez-faire norms, the Supreme Court weakened the powers of the ICC in various ways. Perhaps the most important setback was an 1896 ruling that the ICC had no authority to set railroad rates, a decision that left this responsibility with the carriers. Whatever its shortcomings, the ICC was the first federal regulatory agency and heralded the rise of the administrative state during the twentieth century.

State taxation of goods moving in interstate commerce also proved vexing for the Supreme Court. In *Woodruff v. Parham* (1869) the justices ruled that states could levy a sales tax on all goods sold, including those imported from other jurisdictions. The Court realized, however, that the use of state taxing power might interfere with interstate commerce, and so it was quick to strike down discriminatory taxes designed to insulate local businesses from competition. Hence, in *Welton v. Missouri* (1875) the justices found a license tax imposed only on peddlers who sold goods manufactured outside Missouri to be an unconstitutional encroachment on federal authority under the commerce clause. Thereafter, the Court repeatedly held that states could not place discriminatory taxes on out-of-state goods or charge discriminatory license fees.

As Congress began gingerly to regulate interstate commerce, the Supreme Court adopted a restrictive conception of commerce and thereby limited the reach of Congress under the commerce clause. In *Kidd v. Pearson* (1888) the justices concluded that a state could prevent the manufacture of liquor for shipment to other states. Distinguishing between commerce and production, the Court defined commerce as trade and transportation. Under this interpretation, only the states could regulate manufacturing, mining, and agriculture. Although the distinction between commerce and production was later attacked as artificial, it preserved extensive state control over business and was broadly consistent with the constitutional scheme granting enumerated powers to Congress.

The full implications of *Kidd* became evident in cases dealing with antitrust policy. Widespread public concern about monopolistic practices and market domination by a handful of powerful corporations led to passage of the Sherman Antitrust Act of 1890 which declared illegal every contract or combination in restraint of trade among the states. At issue in *United States v. E. C. Knight Co.* (1895) was an effort by the government to dissolve a combination which controlled over 90 percent of the sugar refining in the country and was thus able to control the price of sugar. Speaking for the Court, Chief Justice Melville W. Fuller forcefully asserted: "Commerce succeeds to manufacture, and is not part of it."[21] Because the refining of sugar was manufacturing rather than commerce, such activity could not be governed by the Sherman Act. Fuller further differentiated between "direct" and "indirect" effects on commerce. He conceded that a monopoly enterprise that had a direct impact on interstate commerce was subject to federal control, but argued that manufacturing monopolies had only an indirect effect. The *Knight* decision limited the scope of the Sherman Act and reflected a strong desire to maintain the traditional role of the states in controlling manufacturing and agriculture.

Likewise, the Supreme Court narrowly construed congressional taxing authority. By the 1890s, industrialization was producing growing disparities of wealth. Anxious to reduce concentrations of wealth and to enhance federal revenue, many in Congress favored placing a larger share of the tax burden on the wealthy. After a bitter debate, Congress in 1894 enacted a second income tax, placing a levy of 2 percent on individual and corporate income over $4000 a year. Promoted by Democrats, the income tax provision was designed to offset the revenue loss resulting from a reduction in the tariff on imports. Only a handful of individuals concentrated in the Northeast were affected by the tax. Thus, the imposition of an income tax had sectional as well as class implications.

An income tax was especially suspect under the precepts of laissez-faire constitutionalism because it represented class legislation that burdened only one segment of society. Critics also feared that the tax was the opening wedge for additional assaults on property rights. Conservatives promptly arranged a challenge to the newly enacted levy in *Pollock v. Farmers' Loan & Trust Co.* (1895). The case aroused keen emotions on all sides. Arguing before the Supreme Court, Joseph H. Choate, a prominent New York attorney, characterized the income tax "as communistic in its purposes and tendencies." He further asserted that this case involved "the preservation of the fundamental rights of private property and equality before the law."[22]

Such arguments found their mark. Writing for a six-to-two majority in *Pollock,* Chief Justice Fuller held that the tax on income from land was a direct tax that was not apportioned among the states according to population, as required by the Constitution. To reach this conclusion, Fuller distinguished the earlier *Springer* decision upholding the Civil War income tax. In addition, the Court unanimously found that the tax on income from municipal bonds was unconstitutional because the federal government could not tax state bonds. The Court was divided four to four on the validity of the tax on general incomes, and the case was reargued when the absent justice could be present. In the second *Pollock* decision, a five-to-four majority overturned the entire income tax as an unconstitutional direct tax.

The income tax controversy sharply divided both the Court and the nation. As Justice Field's concurring opinion demonstrates, the majority was moved to safeguard property interests against perceived spoliation by the political majority. Declaring that the entire tax was void, Field darkly warned of class struggle: "The present assault upon capital is but the beginning. It will be but the stepping-stone to others, larger and more sweeping, till our political contests will become a war of the poor against the rich."[23] The dissenters denied that the income tax discriminated against the wealthy and charged that the majority was frustrating political democracy. Justice Henry Brown decried the decision as "nothing less than a surrender of the taxing power to the moneyed class."[24]

Sorely disappointed, reformers stridently attacked the Supreme Court for usurping political authority. Unquestionably the Court in *Pollock* went out of its way to uphold property rights in the face of redistributionist sentiments. Still, as Lawrence M. Friedman has pointed out, the Court's "instincts were rather shrewd."[25] The justices perceived that an income tax would indeed greatly increase federal revenue and power and would portend further moves to reallocate wealth in a more egalitarian fashion.

The Gilded Age marked an important watershed in American constitutional history. The Supreme Court progressively enlarged its scrutiny of state regulatory legislation in order to safeguard economic rights. Under economic due process, the courts viewed regulation with suspicion and required legislators to justify restrictions on economic liberty. Freedom to use property and enter contracts was treated as the norm. Yet it would be misleading to understand the Supreme Court as motivated simply by a desire to promote the interests of business and property owners. In fact, the Court was ambivalent toward economic regulations and used judicial review selectively. The justices tended to strike down redistributive or class legislation but found that most exercises of the police power passed muster.

Furthermore, the growing commitment to laissez-faire principles never found universal acceptance. Reformers called on government to curb private economic power and to assist actively the disadvantaged. In 1892 the Populists championed the nationalization of the railroads, the breakup of monopolies, a graduated income tax, and currency policies to help debtors. Although this radical Populist program was never completely adopted, it foreshadowed greater governmental regulation of the economy in the twentieth century.

Certain themes stand out in the Supreme Court's supervision of economic legislation. First, by imposing constitutional standards on the rate-fixing process and the payment of municipal bonds, the justices sought to protect the accumulation of investment capital necessary for economic growth. Second, by reviewing the substantive reasonableness of regulations and striking down class legislation, the Court protected entrepreneurs from unduly onerous restrictions and from laws operating to the advantage of particular groups. Third, by invalidating state regulations that blocked interstate commerce, the Court showed its determination to defend the national market against parochial state-imposed obstructions. This laissez-faire constitutionalism harmonized with the prevailing entrepreneurial ethic of the Gilded Age. It would be sorely tested in the early twentieth century, as the demand for effective public control of giant corporations and redress of economic grievances grew more insistent.

6

Progressive Reform and Judicial Conservatism, 1900–1932

By 1900 the United States had become the foremost industrial nation in the world. A new industrial and urban society increasingly supplanted the older America of rural communities. Although many Americans prospered during the early decades of the twentieth century, the tremendous economic expansion caused social dislocation. As businesses became larger, employment relations were fundamentally altered. Employees of corporations frequently worked in an impersonal environment and had little bargaining power to determine their working conditions. Few employees were members of labor unions, and consequently employers could effectively dictate the terms of employment. Cities increased rapidly in size as immigrants and farm workers were attracted to new employment opportunities. Local governments confronted overcrowded housing and public health problems. The proximity of manufacturing operations and residential areas raised concerns about safety and affected living conditions.

In response to these changed economic conditions, a broad-based reform movement, known as Progressivism, emerged during the early years of the twentieth century. The objectives of this coalition were diverse and included electoral reforms designed to make the political system more responsive to the public. But the primary Progressive concern was to correct the imbalance of economic power associated with the new industrial order. Contending that the unregulated market often functioned poorly, Progressives sought to control large-scale corporate enterprise in order to preserve competition and mitigate the conditions of industrial employment. At the heart of the reform program lay the Progressive insistence on a more active role for both state and federal governments in regulating the economy and meeting social problems.

Progressives viewed the states as important laboratories for legislative experimentation. Indeed, they enjoyed considerable success at the state level, persuading legislators to enact a wide range of statutes protecting employees in the workplace. Such legislation included the creation of workmen's compensation to aid workers injured in the factory, the imposition of safety and health standards, and the passage of laws setting the maximum number of working hours and establishing minimum wages. These measures necessarily curtailed contractual freedom and the right of owners to use their property. Thus the Progressives championed an expansive reading of state police power to provide a constitutional basis for this protective legislation. Under the tenets of laissez-faire constitutionalism, however, wages and working conditions were ordinarily determined by the operation of the free market.

Influenced by laissez-faire values, the majority of Supreme Court justices remained leery of economic regulations that altered free-market ordering or infringed on property rights. In the seminal case of *Lochner v. New York* (1905) the Court gave sharp teeth to economic due process by invalidating a statute that restricted work in bakeries to ten hours a day or sixty hours a week.[1] Speaking for a five-to-four majority, Justice Rufus W. Peckham held that the law violated the liberty of contract as protected by the Fourteenth Amendment. Although he recognized that a state could enact laws to protect the health of workers, Peckham was not persuaded that the baking trade was unhealthy. He could find no direct relationship between the number of working hours and the health of bakers. Peckham reasoned that "the real object and purpose" of the statute was to regulate labor relations rather than the purported end of safeguarding health. Because Peckham felt that bakers were fully capable of asserting their interests and were "in no sense wards of the State," he described statutes limiting hours of work "as mere meddlesome interferences with the rights of the individual."[2] Therefore, he concluded that the statute exceeded the permissible bounds of state police power. Peckham also expressed broad disapproval of labor protective legislation. "It is impossible for us to shut our eyes," he wrote, "to the fact that many of the laws of this character, while passed under what is claimed to be the police power for the purpose of protecting the public health or welfare, are, in reality, passed from other motives.''[3]

Two dissenters attacked the majority's position from different perspectives. Justice John M. Harlan accepted the legitimacy of the liberty of contract doctrine but argued that the Court misapplied it in this case. Emphasizing that contracts were subject to health and safety regulations, he maintained that long hours of work in bakeries endangered the health of employees. Hence the legislature was justified in enacting the statute. Justice Oliver Wendell Holmes went a step further and rejected the laissez-faire interpretation of the Constitution. "This case," he charged, "is decided upon an economic theory which a large part of the country does not entertain."[4] Holmes articulated a philosophy of judicial restraint under which the Court should defer to "the right of a majority to embody their opinions in law."[5] Skeptical about absolute legal values, Holmes sought to preserve a wide latitude for the political resolution of economic disputes.

The *Lochner* decision firmly established the Supreme Court's authority to review the substance of economic regulations under the due process clause. For the next thirty years the Court closely scrutinized the reasonableness of numerous statutes affecting property rights. The Court treated liberty of contract as the general rule governing economic affairs. State interference with this right under the police power could be justified only in exceptional circumstances, and such restraint could not be arbitrary. Moreover, as demonstrated in *Lochner,* the justices did not accept at face value the ostensible rationale advanced to explain the exercise of the police power. To the discomfort of the Progressives, the *Lochner* decision became a symbol of the Supreme Court's commitment to property rights.

Despite the triumph of laissez-faire constitutionalism, the outcome in *Lochner* did not bar all legislative reform. The Supreme Court was receptive to laws dealing with obvious health and safety risks even when such regulations imposed heavy costs on property owners or businesses. For instance, the justices upheld the regulation of safety in mines and workmen compensation statutes that provided for a financial award to employees injured by industrial accidents. Indeed, the Supreme Court seemingly retreated from *Lochner* by upholding state laws that controlled working hours. The Court also took a deferential view with respect to state supervision of public morals. Thus, the justices readily approved laws restricting the operation of lotteries and pool halls and prohibiting the manufacture and sale of alcoholic beverages. Nor did the Supreme Court see any constitutional infirmity with laws to prevent fraudulent business practices.

In order to demonstrate the reasonableness of economic regulation, the Progressives developed a fresh manner of understanding law. Rejecting the notion that legal principles were fixed, reformers demanded that law reflect social reality and the underlying needs of society. They called for a connection between law and the insights of social science. Louis D. Brandeis was among the most influential proponents of this sociological jurisprudence. A successful corporate attorney with a Boston practice, Brandeis was an articulate advocate of Progressivism. He argued that the courts should take account of economic and social changes and consider the validity of regulatory legislation in light of contemporary social conditions.

To give practical application to these reformist attitudes, Brandeis pioneered the use of social facts before the courts. He fashioned the so-called Brandeis brief in which nonlegal materials such as medical information, health data, factory inspection reports, and economic statistics were presented to judges in order to justify legislative regulation of working conditions. The Brandeis brief was designed to encourage judges to avoid relying solely on legal precedent in reviewing legislation and to prevent the mechanical application of the liberty of contract doctrine. It also initiated a broader practice in which judges increasingly considered the social context of lawsuits when passing on constitutional issues.

Brandeis successfully used this approach in *Muller v. Oregon* (1908). At issue was a state law that limited the number of working hours for women in factories and laundries to ten hours a day. Unanimously sustaining this measure, the Supreme Court stressed the special health needs of women and their dependent status as justifying disparate treatment under law. The justices did not see women as equal competitors with men in the marketplace and thus accepted the necessity for protective legislation. Although a qualified victory for reform, *Muller* did not repudiate *Lochner* or challenge the dominance of economic due process. Moreover, the paternalistic assumptions behind Progressive legislation designed to protect women appear suspect to modern eyes. Often these laws had the effect of placing women at a disadvantage in securing employment and pigeonholing them in particular occupations.

Notwithstanding this willingness to accommodate some regulation of economic life, the Supreme Court increasingly relied on the doctrines of economic due process and liberty of contract to safeguard property rights. In general terms, the Court rejected those regulations that it deemed excessive or unwarranted. The contours of such review were imprecise, but the Court tended to look with disfavor on several types of economic legislation: labor laws, anticompetitive measures, and statutes fixing wages and prices.

The Supreme Court felt that government should not intervene in labor–management relations. This attitude was illustrated by a line of cases that struck down both federal and state laws prohibiting the so-called yellow dog contract. Such contracts made it a term of employment that employees not belong to labor unions. Widespread use of these agreements seriously hampered the union movement in the early twentieth century. Finding that the laws banning yellow dog contracts had no reasonable relationship to public health and safety, the Supreme Court ruled that such statutes were an arbitrary interference with the right of employers and employees to contract concerning employment conditions. These decisions were bitterly resented by union leaders and social reformers, who accused the Court of harboring an antiunion bias and siding with employers.

Although the justices may have held unrealistic notions about the bargaining position of individual employees, allegations of systematic favoritism to business are difficult to demonstrate. In actuality the Supreme Court was committed to the laissez-faire norm of an unregulated market economy. Thus, the justices also invalidated laws restricting the right to engage in business or imposing barriers to new enterprises. For example, in *Adams v. Tanner* (1917) the Supreme Court, by a six-to-three vote, overturned a Washington statute that in effect prevented employment agencies from conducting business. The justices determined that the law unduly limited the right to engage in a useful business as protected by the due process clause. Similarly, the Court invalidated a New York law that curtailed the practice of ticket scalping.

Even more revealing was the decision in *New State Ice Co. v. Liebmann* (1932), which vividly confirmed the Supreme Court's devotion to free-market competition. Oklahoma declared the manufacture and sale of ice to be a business affected with a public interest and required a certificate for entering the ice business. To obtain such a certificate an applicant had to show "necessity" and the inadequacy of existing facilities. The Court emphasized that the practical effect of the certificate provision was to shut out new enterprises and thus foster a monopoly in the existing ice companies. Accordingly, the Court, by a margin of six to two, found that the Oklahoma statute unreasonably curtailed the right to engage in a lawful private business in violation of the due process clause. Brandeis, now a member of the Supreme Court, dissented. He argued that economic competition in some circumstances could be wasteful and destructive and therefore that the state should enjoy discretion in controlling entry into the ice business. These rulings suggest that the paramount concern of the justices was to protect entrepreneurial liberty.

In another series of cases the Supreme Court sharply limited the authority of government to regulate wages and prices. During the Gilded Age the Court had recognized the power of the states to control the prices charged by businesses impressed with a public interest, such as railroads and utilities, as long as such regulated rates produced a fair return for investors. Legislative attempts to set minimum wages, however, raised novel issues. The justices were loath to accept wage regulation or to expand the category of businesses in which wage or price fixing was constitutional. In the leading case of *Adkins v. Children's Hospital* (1923) the Supreme Court, by a five-to-three margin, overruled a District of Columbia statute that established a minimum wage for women as an infringement of the liberty of contract. Speaking for the Court, Justice George Sutherland stressed that "freedom of contract is . . . the general rule and restraint the exception."[6] Distinguishing wage laws from measures limiting the hours of labor, he reasoned that the minimum wage law arbitrarily cast on employers a welfare function that rightly belonged to society at large. Characterizing the minimum wage law as a price-fixing measure, Sutherland argued that the law disregarded the "moral requirement" of an equivalence between the value of labor and wages. In a forceful dissent, Chief Justice William Howard Taft contended that lawmakers could limit freedom of contract under the police power to regulate the maximum number of hours or the minimum wages of women. He cautioned that the justices should not invalidate regulatory statutes simply because they deem such economic policies to be unwise.

Adkins was a clear expression of laissez-faire constitutionalism, and demonstrated a strong belief that wage and price determinations rested with business owners and employees. The same philosophy guided the Court in striking down a compulsory wage arbitration scheme on liberty of contract grounds. Thus, in *Charles Wolff Packing Company v. Court of Industrial Relations of Kansas* (1923) the justices ruled that a mere legislative declaration that a business was affected with a public interest was not sufficient to alter the legal status of a private enterprise and subject it to regulation.

Moreover, the Supreme Court continued to protect investors even in those industries in which price regulation was constitutionally permissible. In *Smyth v. Ames* (1898) it required that utility rates be based on the current value of a company's assets. However, inflation during World War I caused the current value of utility property to increase dramatically. Consequently, the effect of the *Smyth* rule was virtually to undercut the states' ability to control railroad or utility rates. During the 1920s the *Smyth* rule became controversial, but the Supreme Court adhered to this approach in *Missouri ex rel Southwestern Bell Telephone Co. v. Public Service Commission* (1923). In a concurring opinion, Brandeis and Holmes agreed that the rate under review was confiscatory, but they argued that the states should be free to adopt as a rate base the value of prudently invested property.

In addition to safeguarding the free market, the Supreme Court sometimes treated economic rights and other liberties as interdependent. For instance, the judicial protection of property rights was instrumental in a successful assault on residential segregation laws. Like many communities, Louisville, Kentucky, enacted an ordinance forbidding black persons from occupying houses in neighborhoods in which the majority of homes were occupied by whites. The city attempted to justify this measure as an exercise of the police power to promote racial harmony. Writing for a unanimous Supreme Court in *Buchanan v. Warley* (1917), Justice William Day broadly declared: "Property is more than the mere thing which a person owns. It is elementary that it includes the right to acquire, use, and dispose of it."[7] He held that this restriction on the right to alienate property constituted a deprivation of property without due process. In *Buchanan,* the defense of property rights produced a libertarian victory against racial discrimination. Similarly, in *Pierce v. Society of Sisters* (1925) the Court overturned an Oregon statute that required parents to educate their children in a public school. This measure, Justice James C. McReynolds stated, interfered with both the liberty of parents and the property rights of private schools.

While seeking reform at the state level, the Progressives also called on the federal government to play an active role in regulating the economy. In particular, they urged Congress to expand the use of federal power to eliminate social ills and control the competitive behavior of large corporations. Reformers took particular aim at lotteries, monopolistic practices, the sale of adulterated food, and child labor. Yet the prevailing understanding of federal commerce power hampered reform efforts. During the late nineteenth century the Supreme Court drew a distinction between commerce and manufacturing, thus placing control of production beyond the power of Congress. The Court cautiously recognized a greater scope for federal authority over commerce but continued to insist that important areas of economic life could not be governed by Congress.

The Supreme Court enlarged in several ways the reach of federal power under the commerce clause. First, in *Champion v. Ames* (1903) a five-to-four majority of the Court upheld a federal statute prohibiting the transportation of lottery tickets in interstate commerce. Congress was clearly seeking to protect public morals rather than simply to regulate commercial transactions. Speaking for the Court, Justice John M. Harlan maintained that Congress had broad authority to exclude articles deemed harmful from interstate commerce. In effect the Court recognized the existence of a federal police power, thus allowing Congress to enter fields that hitherto had been in the states' exclusive domain. Taking prompt advantage of this newly established power, Congress in 1906 banned the shipment of adulterated foods in interstate commerce.

Second, the justices strengthened federal regulatory power by adopting the stream of commerce doctrine. In *Swift and Co. v. United States* (1905) the Court unanimously held that the operation of stockyards, although local in nature, was an integral part of "a current of commerce among the states" because the meat products were shipped to other states. Hence, the antitrust laws could constitutionally be applied to the stockyards. The stream-of-commerce doctrine softened the barrier between manufacturing and commerce. In subsequent cases the Court sustained federal regulations in which local economic activity was inextricably tied to interstate transportation.

Third, the Supreme Court affirmed efforts by the Interstate Commerce

Commission to control intrastate commerce when it adversely affected interstate commerce. In the Hepburn Act of 1906, Congress expressly empowered the ICC to fix interstate railroad rates. At issue in the *Shreveport Rate Case* (1914) was a conflict between federal and state rates for transporting goods to places in east Texas. The charges for shipments from Shreveport, Louisiana, were higher than the rates for shipping the same distance within Texas. To alleviate this discrimination against interstate commerce, the ICC directed the railroads to adjust their rates and permitted the Texas carriers to increase their intrastate charges. Upholding this order, Justice Charles Evans Hughes explained: "Wherever the interstate and intrastate transactions of carriers are so related that the government of the one involves the control of the other, it is Congress, and not the State, that is entitled to prescribe the final and dominant rule."[8] This decision significantly expanded congressional power over state rate-setting authority.

Despite this gradual extension of congressional power under the commerce clause, the Supreme Court did not recognize comprehensive federal control over all segments of the economy. The justices continued to distinguish sharply between interstate and intrastate commerce. In *The Employers' Liability Cases* (1908), for example, the Court held that a carrier engaged in interstate commerce did not submit its local business operations to federal control. Therefore, Congress could abolish the fellow-servant rule for railroad employees working in interstate commerce, but not for those whose duties had no relation to interstate commerce.

Far more controversial, however, was the Supreme Court's decision in *Hammer v. Dagenhart* (1918) which invalidated a statute banning from interstate commerce the shipment of goods produced in a plant that used child labor. A five-to-four majority reasoned that the products of child labor, unlike adulterated food, were not inherently harmful. The Court then concluded that Congress was in fact seeking to control factory employment rather than interstate commerce. Because manufacturing was not regarded as part of commerce, this regulation exceeded the power of Congress and invaded state jurisdiction in violation of the Tenth Amendment. In a lively dissent Justice Holmes argued that congressional power to regulate or prohibit interstate commerce was not limited by its indirect effect on state policy. The elimination of child labor was an important goal of the Progressive movement, and so the issue was emotionally charged.[9] Consequently, the *Hammer* decision was widely condemned and remains difficult to justify to modern readers. Perhaps the ruling can best be understood as a manifestation of the Supreme Court's long-standing commitment to federalism and the existing balance between state and federal authority over economic matters. Writing for the majority, Justice William R. Day warned that "if Congress can thus regulate matters entrusted to local authority by prohibition of the movement of commodities in interstate commerce, all freedom of commerce will be at an end, and the power of the States over local matters may be eliminated, and thus our system of government practically destroyed."[10]

To implement social and economic reforms, the Progressive movement championed the growth of the administrative state. Reformers placed great faith in the administrative approach to regulatory issues. As envisioned by Progressives, independent regulatory agencies composed of nonpolitical experts would exercise sound judgment in carrying out legislative policy. Regulation by means of administration agencies offered the advantages of expertise and flexibility and promised a rational, scientific method of controlling business activity. Following the example of the Interstate Commerce Commission, Congress during the early twentieth century created a host of new administrative commissions and agencies to regulate aspects of the economy. Thus, in 1913 Congress created the Federal Reserve Board to oversee banking and credit and, a year later, established the Federal Trade Commission (FTC) to police unfair trade practices.

This novel regulatory approach was not without problems. In retrospect at least, the Progressives' confidence in the nonpartisan and scientific character of the administrative agencies seems naive. Issues of economic policy invariably had a political dimension. Moreover, Congress often passed only general legislation that set no definite guidelines for administrative implementation. In effect, Congress delegated legislative power to the agencies to determine the substance of regulatory standards. This raised troublesome questions of democratic accountability and the separation of powers. Despite these shortcomings, the administrative agencies proved valuable to solving economic problems, and they remain one of the Progressives' most enduring contributions to constitutional development.

Congressional taxing powers were also strengthened in the early twentieth century. The Supreme Court approved the use of taxation to regulate or prohibit economic activity that could not be reached directly by Congress under the commerce clause. For example, in *McCray v. United States* (1904) the Court upheld the imposition of a prohibitory tax on yellow oleomargarine. Although the obvious purpose of this tax was not to raise revenue but to assist the dairy industry by suppressing oleomargarine, the justices declined to consider the motivation of Congress in passing the levy. Because the taxing power was not limited to interstate commerce, the *McCray* decision seemingly permitted Congress to regulate all aspects of the economy. Indeed, to protect employee health, in 1912 Congress levied a prohibitive excise tax on phosphorus matches, thereby forcing the industry to abandon the use of phosphorus for match heads.

Any expectations for the broad use of tax authority to achieve regulatory ends were soon dashed. After the Supreme Court struck down the child labor law in *Hammer,* Congress turned to the taxing power in an effort to circumvent the decision. To halt the use of child labor, Congress placed a 10 percent tax on the profits of companies employing children. In *Bailey v. Drexel Furniture Co.* (1922) the Supreme Court scrutinized the purpose behind the tax measure and held, by an eight-to-one margin, that the child labor tax was an unconstitutional infringement on state authority to regulate manufacturing. "To give such magic to the word 'tax,'" Chief Justice Taft observed, "would be to break down all constitutional limitations of the powers of Congress and completely wipe out the sovereignty of the States."[11] Although Taft sought to distinguish the *McCray* case, the result of the *Bailey* ruling was to curtail the use of the taxing power for regulatory purposes.

Although disappointing to child labor reformers, the *Bailey* decision was not a surprise to most observers. Indeed, the outcome harmonized with the conservative and entrepreneurial spirit of the 1920s. Reformers turned to a proposed constitutional amendment as a means of eliminating child labor. Congress proposed such an amendment in 1924, but the ratification campaign failed in the face of public hostility to enlarged federal regulation of an area traditionally under state control.

In contrast to the restrictive result in *Bailey,* the authority of Congress to tax incomes was expressly established by adoption of the Sixteenth Amendment in 1913. There was renewed pressure after 1900 to enact an income tax to break up concentrated wealth. Seeking to defeat a direct challenge to the *Pollock* decision, Senate conservatives in 1909 proposed a constitutional amendment enabling Congress to tax incomes without apportionment among the states according to population. They mistakenly calculated that the proposal would fail to win ratification by the states. The Sixteenth Amendment voided the *Pollock* decision, and Congress promptly used its new power to levy a graduated tax on individual incomes over $3000 as well as corporate income. The taxation of income rapidly became the principal source of revenue for the federal government and in fact was instrumental in financing America's involvement in World War I. In the long run the Sixteenth Amendment fundamentally altered the constitutional scheme. It breached the laissez-faire protection of property rights by opening the door for tax policies designed to redistribute wealth. Moreover, it provided a financial base from which the federal government greatly extended its reach.

In addition to considering the scope of congressional power to regulate and tax, the Supreme Court faced new questions concerning the protection of property rights under the takings clause of the Fifth Amendment. Urbanization and industrialization created serious land use problems in the years after 1900. As a consequence, both the federal government and the states began to control more vigorously the use of land. Yet government restrictions on the use of privately owned property raised difficult constitutional questions. Landowners increasingly complained that the cost of achieving new social measures was unfairly and unconstitutionally placed on their shoulders rather than imposed on the general public. During the Gilded Age the Supreme Court rejected arguments that regulations limiting the utilization of property constituted a taking for which the payment of compensation was required.

In the early twentieth century, however, the Supreme Court reconsidered that position and broadened the protection of landowners under the takings clause. In *Pennsylvania Coal Co. v. Mahon* (1922) the Court recognized the concept of a regulatory taking in which the value or usefulness of private property was unduly diminished by governmental action. A transfer of title or a physical incursion was unnecessary for a taking to occur. Justice Holmes formulated the crucial inquiry in *Mahon:* "The general rule at least is, that while property may be regulated to a certain extent, if regulation goes too far it will be recognized as a taking."[12] Although noting that the state police power could limit the use of property, Holmes cautioned that "the natural tendency of human nature" was to extend the qualification "until at last private property disappears."[13]

The landmark *Mahon* case arose out of coal mining practices in Pennsylvania. A mining company sold land but expressly reserved the right to remove all the coal beneath the surface and placed the risk of subsidence on the purchasers. Over time many persons erected dwellings on this land and faced the prospect of a cave-in if the mining company removed the subterranean support. Responding to this problem, the Pennsylvania legislature enacted the Kohler Act, which prohibited mining in such a way as to cause a residence to collapse. The mining company challenged the constitutionality of this measure, arguing that the statute constituted an uncompensated taking of its property right to remove coal. Speaking for the Supreme Court, Justice Holmes agreed that the regulation was so extreme as to constitute a seizure of property without just compensation. He pointed out that Pennsylvania could achieve its objectives by exercising eminent domain and using tax funds to pay for the restrictions imposed on the mining company. Although the *Mahon* decision established that a land use regulation might be deemed a taking, it remained difficult to distinguish between appropriate restrictions and an unconstitutional taking. The Court was reluctant to apply the doctrine of regulatory taking.

Another vexing issue was raised by the emergence of zoning as a land control technique. Urbanization produced congested living conditions, and consequently an owner's use of land had a direct bearing on his neighbor's property and quality of life. When traditional nuisance law proved inadequate to cope with urban land use problems, localities began to enact specific restrictions to safeguard public health and safety. In *Welch v. Swasey* (1909) the Supreme Court had no difficulty in unanimously affirming a Boston ordinance that limited the height of buildings. New York City enacted America's first comprehensive zoning ordinance in 1916, and zoning proliferated during the 1920s. Under the leadership of Herbert Hoover, the United States Department of Commerce encouraged the adoption of zoning plans. Zoning was justified as an exercise of the police power to protect the public. But such regulations restricted an owner's dominion over his land and often impaired its value. Critics argued that zoning represented an unconstitutional interference with the right of owners to use their property.

In *Village of Euclid v. Ambler Realty Company* (1926) the Court, by a six-to-three vote, upheld the constitutionality of a comprehensive zoning ordinance that divided a locality into districts, residential and commercial, thereby restricting the type of building construction in each district. Reasoning that such limitations served the health, safety, and morals of the public, Justice Sutherland ruled that state police power included the authority to classify land and prevent the erection of commercial buildings in residential areas. To bolster its decision the Court drew an analogy between zoning and the power to abate a common law nuisance.

It is something of a paradox why, at a time when the Supreme Court readily overturned legislation regulating business, the justices were so receptive to early land use controls. The *Euclid* opinion contains some clues. Justice Sutherland believed that zoning would enhance the value of land. In this regard, he pointedly observed that apartment houses could be excluded from single-family residential areas. These views help explain the popularity of zoning. From the outset many property owners perceived that zoning served their interests by stabilizing land values, imposing income segregation, and preventing undesirable land uses. Seen in this light, the *Euclid* decision helped preserve property rights generally even if individual landowners suffered a loss. Of course, during the 1920s, zoning was in its infancy, and the full implications of land use regulation were not yet apparent.

Moreover, the Court stressed that the zoning power was not unfettered. In *Nectow v. City of Cambridge* (1928) the Supreme Court struck down a particular application of a zoning ordinance as a deprivation of property without due process. Writing for the Court, Justice Sutherland declared: "The governmental power to interfere by zoning regulations with the general rights of the land owner by restricting the character of his use, is not unlimited, and . . . such restriction cannot be imposed if it does not bear a substantial relation to the public health, safety, morals, or general welfare."[14] This approach contemplated judicial inquiry as to whether zoning regulations were actually related to public health and safety.

The regulation of rent and rental practices was also a source of controversy. Citing emergency housing conditions growing out of World War I, a congressional measure established a commission to determine reasonable rents in the District of Columbia and protected a tenant's right of occupancy. This regulation obviously limited the right of the property owner to determine rental charges for occupancy of his land. By a vote of five to four, the Supreme Court in *Block v. Hirsh* (1921) upheld the validity of the statute. Observing that "public exigency will justify the legislature in restricting property rights in land to a certain extent without compensation,"[15] Justice Holmes concluded that under the circumstances of a wartime housing shortage, the rental business in the District was cloaked with a public interest justifying temporary regulation. Suggesting an analogy between renting property and public utilities, Holmes noted that the power to regulate rates was well established.

In a vigorous dissent Chief Justice Edward D. White found the statute to constitute an uncompensated taking in violation of the Fifth Amendment. Asserting that "the security of property, next to personal security against exertions of government, is of the essence of liberty," he strongly denied that constitutional safeguards were suspended during a purported emergency.[16] According to White, the statute improperly transferred dominion over rental property from the landlord to the tenant, and he expressed fear that the outcome in this case would encourage similar measures elsewhere. Indeed, the *Block* decision set the stage for the gradual spread of rent control.

The most sweeping destruction of property rights during this period occurred as a result of Prohibition. Advocates of Prohibition gained powerful political force in the early years of the twentieth century. By 1916 nineteen states had enacted statewide prohibition acts, and many cities and counties in other jurisdictions forbad the sale of liquor under local option laws. During World War I Congress passed several laws banning the use of foodstuffs for the production of alcoholic beverages. Challenges to these wartime statutes, however, were unavailing. The Supreme Court validated the measures as an exercise of Congress's war power. Ratification of the Eighteenth Amendment in 1919 marked the culmination of a long drive to halt the manufacture and sale of intoxicating liquors. Prohibition inflicted economic hardship on the owners of breweries and distilleries: They suffered a sharp drop in the value of their property and experienced a total loss of the stock on hand when Prohibition became effective.

Although the Supreme Court employed various techniques to safeguard economic interests, the contract clause played only a minor role. Indeed, the Court steadily heard fewer challenges to state legislation based on the contract clause. Further, the justices tended to take a narrow view of contract clause protection. At issue in *Manigault v. Springs* (1905), for instance, was an agreement between private parties to leave a navigable creek unobstructed. Then a later state statute authorized one of the parties to construct a dam. Rejecting the contention that this law impaired the obligation of contract, the Supreme Court held that private contracts could be affected by exercise of the police power. Yet if contractual arrangements could be modified whenever the state deemed it necessary, the contract clause afforded little protection to the contracting parties. Although during the 1920s the Court relied on the contract clause in several cases to invalidate state regulations, the provision did not occupy a place of importance in constitutional thought.

Throughout this period, reformers viewed the federal judiciary as an obstacle to their program. Corrective social and economic legislation was difficult to achieve as long as the Supreme Court extended significant constitutional protection to the rights of property owners and particularly to corporate enterprise. A leading Progressive, Senator Robert M. LaFollette of Wisconsin, forcefully expressed this sentiment: "Gradually the judiciary began to loom up as the one formidable obstacle which must be overcome before anything substantial could be accomplished to free the public from the exactions of oppressive monopolies and from the domination of property interests."[17] Accordingly, the Progressives leveled a series of complaints against the Supreme Court and the prevailing doctrine of laissez-faire constitutionalism.

First, scholars associated with the Progressive movement sought to undermine the aura of sanctity surrounding the Constitution and the Supreme Court. Foremost among this intellectual challenge was the publication in 1913 of Charles A. Beard's *An Economic Interpretation of the Constitution of the United States*.[18] Beard pictured the drafting of the Constitution in conspiratorial tones. The framers of the Constitution, he contended, were wealthy property owners who had a personal stake in protecting property rights and checking majority rule. Although Beard's analysis has been sharply challenged by later historians, the immediate effect of this controversial work was to call into question the neutrality of constitutional adjudication.

Second, the Progressives asserted that laissez-faire constitutionalism gave the Supreme Court vast discretion over the validity of social and economic measures. Progressives maintained that federal judges were simply substituting their economic views for the judgment of popularly elected legislatures, a practice contrary to the fundamental premises of a democratic society. Even worse, many critics saw the judiciary as permeated with class bias. Federal judges, they charged, were serving the interests of the wealthy and the business community by frustrating legislative efforts at economic reform.

Another line of attack on laissez-faire constitutionalism stressed the unpredictable nature of such jurisprudence. It was difficult to ascertain the distinction between permissible and impermissible regulation. The absence of such lines gave the justices a large reservoir of discretion and seemingly produced inconsistent results. For instance, the Supreme Court invalidated some regulations governing working conditions, but sustained other measures.

The Progressives devised several proposals to curb federal judicial power. Some reformers favored amending the Constitution to strengthen popular control of the judiciary. They suggested the popular election of federal judges and provisions for judicial recall to make the judiciary more responsive to public attitudes. The principal reform prescription, however, was simple: judicial restraint. Progressives favored the position of Justice Holmes that federal judges should defer to the decision of elected lawmakers. Thus, courts should no longer review the reasonableness of economic and social legislation.

In some respects the Progressives' legal critique was overdrawn. The Supreme Court accommodated the reform movement and upheld the majority of regulatory statutes. Moreover, conservative judges genuinely believed that laissez-faire constitutionalism enhanced economic liberty and the opportunity to pursue livelihoods. They also feared that legislative redistribution of wealth would undercut economic growth. In short, judges were not simply handmaidens of the business community. For their part, the Progressives proceeded on the questionable assumption that all social legislation benefited the public. Reformers rarely acknowledged that much economic legislation served selfish special interests.

The results of the reform movement were mixed. Despite the appointment of Brandeis to the Supreme Court in 1916, conservative judges dominated the federal bench throughout the Progressive era. The Court remained skeptical about regulation of the economy, particularly attempts to adjust employment relationships or significantly alter the operations of the free market. None of this, however, should obscure the significant achievement of the Progressive movement in laying the groundwork for a future shift in judicial attitudes. The Progressives planted the seeds of intellectual change that would make judges more receptive to government intervention in the economy. The Progressive view of constitutional law came to fruition when the political climate of the country changed in the 1930s.

In the nineteenth century, steamboats helped to forge a national market. (The Bettmann Archive.)

Farmers bringing grain to a grain elevator in 1879. State regulation of the rates charged by grain elevators was sustained by the Supreme Court in *Munn v. Illinois* (1877). (UPI/Bettmann Newsphotos.)

A pioneer of economic due process, Justice Stephen J. Field consistently championed the rights of property owners in the late nineteenth century. (The Bettmann Archive.)

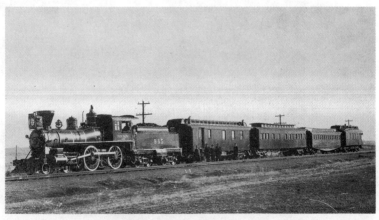

America's first big business, railroads transformed the economy during the nineteenth century and raised vexing issues concerning government control of economic enterprise. (The Bettmann Archive.)

This drawing illustrates a New York City sweat shop in 1885. By the late nineteenth century the states began to regulate workplace conditions. (The Bettmann Archive.)

THE NEW UNCLE SAM.
How the Farmers' Alliance propose to have the Government run when they get the power.

Populist demands for governmental actions to assist farmers challenged laissez-faire values and were ridiculed by conservatives. (*Judge*, January 17, 1891. Courtesy of the Heard Library of Vanderbilt University.)

The 1894 income tax aroused a bitter controversy and was invalidated by the Supreme Court. (*Puck*, May 15, 1895. Courtesy of the Heard Library of Vanderbilt University.)

Reflecting laissez-faire values prevalent in the late nineteenth century, this cartoon satirizes governmental intervention in the economy. (*Puck*, July 14, 1897. Courtesy of the Heard Library of Vanderbilt University.)

A 12 year-old girl working as a spinner in a Vermont cotton mill in 1910. During the early twentieth century the Supreme Court thwarted congressional efforts to eliminate child labor, ruling that only the states had authority to regulate employment in factories. (National Archives.)

Chicago steel strikers in 1919. The extension of federal authority over labor relations was not established until the New Deal era. (UPI/Bettmann Newsphotos.)

During the early twentieth century, Chief Justice William Howard Taft and Justice Oliver Wendell Holmes authored important judicial opinions dealing with commerce and property rights. (The Bettman Archive.)

AND IN THE MEANTIME

UNCLE SAM.—Why don't you throw him that life-preserver? He may be drowning!
THE INTER-STATE COMMERCE COMMISSION. Plenty of time! Let's first make sure that he can't swim.

Regulation of railroad and utility charges potentially constituted a confiscation of property. Taking a sympathetic view of the railroads, this cartoon urges the ICC to authorize a rate increase to preserve the industry's financial position. (*Puck*, June 25, 1913. Courtesy of the Heard Library of Vanderbilt University.)

During the 1920s and 1930s, Justice George Sutherland was a conservative leader on the Supreme Court and a defender of laissez-faire constitutionalism. (UPI/Bettmann Newsphotos.)

During the Great Depression, many farmers feared loss of their farms because of mortgage default. In February 1933, farmers marched on the Nebraska legislature to request enactment of a moratorium on mortgage foreclosures. (Nebraska State Historical Society.)

7

The New Deal and the Demise of Laissez-Faire Constitutionalism

The Great Depression deepened in the 1930s, ushering in an era of economic and political turmoil. Business failures and massive unemployment prompted calls for governmental intervention in the economy. In the face of such severe economic adversity, there was a growing belief that the uncontrolled free market was not functioning well in an industrial society. The election in 1932 of Franklin D. Roosevelt as president, along with a Democratic Congress, marked a watershed in political history. The Republican coalition, which had dominated American political life since the Civil War, was shattered. The new political outlook emphatically rejected the laissez-faire philosophy. Justice Louis D. Brandeis aptly expressed this reform sentiment when he declared in 1932: "There must be power in the States and the Nation to remould, through experimentation, our economic practices and institutions to meet changing social and economic needs."[1]

Borrowing from the Progressive legacy, President Roosevelt's New Deal program was grounded on the notion that government had an affirmative duty to promote the general social welfare. Accordingly, New Deal liberals worked to remedy economic distress, manage the national economy, control corporate behavior, encourage labor unions, and actively promote the economic interests of the disadvantaged. To achieve these objectives, Congress and the states enacted an extraordinary array of measures that greatly enlarged governmental supervision of the economy and sought to redistribute wealth and economic power. This

119

social welfare approach flatly contradicted the insistence on limited governmental activity, marketplace competition, and respect for property rights that were at the heart of laissez-faire constitutionalism.

Despite the marked change in the political landscape, the Supreme Court majority looked with disfavor on most of the New Deal legislation. As matters developed, the justices divided into three camps. Four justices, George Sutherland, Willis Van Devanter, Pierce Butler, and James C. McReynolds, were consistently hostile to New Deal measures. Chief Justice Charles Evans Hughes and Justice Owen J. Roberts were less rigid in their outlook but ordinarily voted with the conservatives. Only Justices Louis D. Brandeis, Harlan F. Stone, and Benjamin N. Cardozo were sympathetic to the New Deal. But even these liberals were suspicious of the trend toward centralization inherent in New Deal policies and joined with the conservative justices on some issues. Consequently, the conservatives were usually able to command a majority in opposition to the New Deal. After a succession of Republican presidents, the lower federal courts were also dominated by judges with conservative political and economic views.

The Supreme Court's stubborn defense of laissez-faire values precipitated a constitutional crisis. Ultimately, under great political pressure and President Roosevelt's threat to "pack" the Court, several justices shifted their position and accommodated the New Deal's economic and social program. As a result of the constitutional revolution of 1937, the Court abandoned laissez-faire constitutionalism and permitted the federal government and the states to play a major role in directing American economic life. Thereafter, the Court relegated property rights to a secondary position and largely turned its attention to other matters.

In the early 1930s many states experimented in fashioning a response to the Great Depression. Lawmakers instituted a variety of relief measures, including price regulations, minimum wage laws, and social welfare programs. The Supreme Court proved surprisingly receptive to these state legislative attempts to mitigate the impact of the depression. Among the problems spawned by the depression was the wholesale loss of homes and farms through foreclosure of delinquent mortgages. At issue in the leading case of *Home Building and Loan Association v. Blaisdell* (1934) was a Minnesota act imposing a limited moratorium on the foreclosure of mortgages. Designed to safeguard the ownership of homes and farms, the statute temporarily suspended the mortgage obligation while allowing the mortgagor to remain in possession upon the payment of a reasonable rent. The mortgage moratorium was similar to debtor-relief laws often declared unconstitutional in the nineteenth century as an impairment of the obligation of contract.

By a five-to-four margin the Supreme Court held that the moratorium did not violate the contract clause. Clearly influenced by the economic emergency, Chief Justice Charles Evans Hughes ruled that contracts were subject to the reasonable exercise of the state police power. The police power encompassed the authority to give temporary relief for extraordinary economic distress. Although susceptible of a narrow construction limiting valid impairments of contracts to emergency situations, Hughes's opinion also suggested in broad terms that the state's interest in regulating economic affairs could justify interference with contracts. Hughes adopted a balancing approach to the interpretation of the contract clause. He weighed the contractual rights of the parties against the public-interest arguments of the state to determine whether the infringement of the mortgage contract was reasonable. In a forceful dissenting opinion Justice George Sutherland maintained that the contract clause was intended to prevent the states from granting debtor relief at the expense of creditors during periods of economic distress. The contract clause, he asserted, "does not contemplate that an emergency shall furnish an occasion for softening the restriction."[2]

Despite the *Blaisdell* decision, the contract clause continued to have some efficacy in the depression era. Indeed, the Supreme Court invalidated several state relief laws between 1934 and 1941 as unconstitutional impairments of contract. For instance, the justices overturned legislation that significantly curtailed the remedies of municipal bondholders in Arkansas, and they voided a statute that altered the rights of purchasers of land titles at tax forfeiture sales. Nonetheless, by enlarging the police power exception the *Blaisdell* opinion hastened the eclipse of the contract clause as a protector of property rights.

Another depression-related concern was declining prices for agricultural products. For decades the dairy industry had lobbied for laws to undercut competition from oleomargarine and to boost milk prices. These efforts intensified during the depression. Responding to such pressure, in 1933 the New York legislature enacted a scheme setting maximum and minimum prices for the retail sale of milk. The milk control law was designed to assist dairy farmers by eliminating price competition and raising the price of milk. It was a clear example of class or special-interest legislation and hence appeared vulnerable to judicial challenge. The Supreme Court had long been hostile to price or wage fixing in private business other than utilities and had often struck down such legislation during the 1920s.

In *Nebbia v. New York* (1934), however, the justices, by a five-to-four vote sustained the milk control law as a reasonable means of stabilizing milk prices. Although obscured by the subsequent controversy over the New Deal program, the *Nebbia* ruling signaled an important shift away from economic due process and judicial supervision of state regulatory legislation. Speaking for the Court, Justice Roberts emphasized that a state could validly "adopt whatever economic policy may reasonably be deemed to promote public welfare." He added: "The Constitution does not guarantee the unrestricted privilege to engage in a business or to conduct it as one pleases."[3] The Court in *Nebbia* effectively enlarged the category of businesses that were subject to state price regulation. Justice McReynolds, in a biting dissent, asserted that the milk control law burdened consumers in order to benefit farmers and constituted an arbitrary interference with entrepreneurial liberty. Consistent with laissez-faire principles, McReynolds contended that the legislature "cannot lawfully destroy guaranteed rights of one man with the prime purpose of enriching another, even if for the moment, this may seem advantageous to the public."[4]

In light of these decisions, the Roosevelt administration was guardedly optimistic that the New Deal economic regulations would pass judicial muster. But reformers' hopes were soon dashed, as the Supreme Court proved decidedly more hostile to congressional efforts to battle the depression and manage the economy under centralized control. In 1935 and 1936 the Court struck down a series of important New Deal measures.

A major source of controversy was the New Deal's heavy reliance on executive and administrative agencies, such as the National Recovery Administration and the Agricultural Adjustment Administration, to regulate the economy and promote recovery. Congress delegated broad rule-making and adjudicatory powers to these agencies but furnished only general guidance as to how such authority should be exercised. In a sense, Congress simply identified the problems and instructed the agencies to devise solutions. The administrators then issued rules and regulations that had the effect of laws. This practice raised the issue of whether Congress had unconstitutionally delegated its legislative function to administrative agencies. It was well settled that Congress could transfer legislative power as long as the statute established adequate standards to govern the exercise of the delegated authority. But the vast scale of the legislative delegation in New Deal measures was without precedent.

The New Deal initially sought business–government cooperation to rebuild the economy. This policy was exemplified by the National Industrial Recovery Act of 1933 (NIRA). Under this act the representatives of large segments of industry were authorized to prepare "codes of fair competition" governing production, prices, and labor relations. Upon approval by the president, these codes had the force of law. Implementation of the codes was entrusted to the National Recovery Administration. Hastily put together in the face of emergency conditions, the NIRA rested on uncertain constitutional underpinnings. Among other difficulties, the NIRA provided no standards to control the president's code-making power.

In *Schechter Poultry Corp. v. United States* (1935) the Supreme Court unanimously overturned the NIRA as an unconstitutional delegation of lawmaking power to the executive branch. The Schechter Poultry Corporation was convicted of violating the live poultry code for New York City. Chief Justice Hughes stressed that "Congress is not permitted to abdicate or to transfer to others the essential legislative functions with which it is thus vested."[5] He found that the NIRA failed to fix standards sufficient to guide the president's discretion in approving codes. Congress, according to Hughes, could not constitutionally delegate to the president the unfetttered discretion to make whatever laws were deemed advisable to promote trade. In addition, the Court was plainly troubled by the fact that the codes were initially drawn up by business groups that could thus serve their own interests. The outcome in *Schechter Poultry Corp.* suggested judicial skepticism regarding the rise of the modern administrative state.

An even more crucial question was the scope of congressional power to regulate business. The New Dealers believed that national economic problems mandated federal solutions. Accordingly, Congress sought to expand federal jurisdiction and moved into fields that had traditionally been reserved for state regulation. The Supreme Court, on the other hand, adhered to the long-established distinction between production and

124   THE GUARDIAN OF EVERY OTHER RIGHT

interstate commerce. According to this view Congress did not possess a comprehensive power over commercial and business activity. In particular, the federal government could not control industrial production or employment conditions in factories. Hence, the Supreme Court in *Schechter Poultry Corp.* also determined that the slaughter and sale of poultry in local markets were not part of interstate commerce. It followed that the code that attempted to set the wages and hours of employees was not a valid exercise of federal commerce power. These matters were reserved for the states under the Tenth Amendment. By confining federal authority to transactions involving the movement of goods across state lines, the Court effectively shielded many businesses from federal regulation.

This line between production and commerce doomed other New Deal initiatives to reform the national economy. In *Carter v. Carter Coal Company* (1936) the Supreme Court, by a vote of six to three, invalidated the Bituminous Coal Conservation Act on grounds that the legislation exceeded the authority of the federal government under the commerce clause. The act established a complex administrative mechanism to regulate coal prices and protected the right of mine workers to organize labor unions. Writing for the Court, Justice Sutherland firmly rejected the contention that the federal government had the implied power to regulate for the general welfare. Emphasizing that production was not part of commerce, he held that "the relation of employer and employee is a local relation."[6] Because the regulation of working conditions was an aspect of production, the federal government could not exercise legislative control. Thus, the *Carter* ruling cast a dark cloud over New Deal attempts to regulate the workplace and encourage collective bargaining by unions.

The Supreme Court also took a restrictive view of congressional power to levy taxes and appropriate money. In an attempt to increase depressed farm prices, the Agricultural Adjustment Act authorized the payment of subsidies to farmers in exchange for reducing the amount of their crops. To raise revenue for this scheme, Congress placed a "processing tax" on the first processor of such commodities. In *United States v. Butler* (1936) the justices, again by a six-to-three margin, struck down the processing tax. Writing for the Court, Justice Roberts concluded that the ostensible tax was in actuality a means of regulating agricultural production, a matter reserved for the states under the Tenth Amendment. Therefore, the levy constituted an unconstitutional "expropriation of money from one group for the benefit of another.''[7] Although he recognized a general power in Congress to tax and spend, Justice Roberts evinced concern about use of the tax power to regulate all aspects of economic life. The outcome in *Butler* was an expression of the laissez-faire preference for limited government.

Yet another objection to the New Deal centered on the takings clause of the Fifth Amendment. To assist indebted farmers, the Frazier–Lemke Act of 1934 compelled the holders of existing mortgages to relinquish farm property to mortgagors without full payment of the mortgage debt. In *Louisville Bank v. Radford* (1935), a unanimous Supreme Court found the act to constitute an unconstitutional taking of property without compensation. Justice Brandeis reasoned that the act attempted to enlarge the rights of debtors by depriving creditors of their security for the mortgage loan. He concluded that the act had taken valuable property rights from mortgage holders. "If the public interest requires . . . the taking of property of individual mortgagees," Justice Brandeis noted, there must be resort to eminent domain "so that, through taxation, the burden of the relief afforded in the public interest may be borne by the public."[8]

In addition to overturning much of the New Deal legislation, the Supreme Court continued to scrutinize state economic regulations. Reaffirming the *Adkins* decision, in 1936 the justices voided a New York minimum wage law for women as a violation of the freedom of contract. This action called into question similar laws in other states and seemingly blocked any federal legislation to increase low wages.

Never before had the Supreme Court struck down so many acts of Congress in such a short period of time. These judicial setbacks dealt a devastating blow to the New Deal program of economic revival and social reform. Further, the line of decisions raised serious questions about the constitutionality of other New Deal measures, including the National Labor Relations Act and the Social Security Act. In their dogged defense of laissez-faire constitutionalism, however, the justices were unmindful of the constraints imposed on the Court by political realities.

The constitutional controversy soon spilled over into the political arena. Conservatives and business leaders praised the Supreme Court as a champion of property rights and individual liberty against New Deal encroachments. In 1936 former President Herbert Hoover extolled the justices for "crashing through New Deal tyrannies" and preventing regimentation of the economy.[9] Like the framers of the Constitution, the defenders of the Court identified property ownership with political freedom. "History furnishes no instance where the right of man to acquire and hold property has been taken away," the renowned attorney John W. Davis wrote, "without the complete destruction of liberty in all its forms."[10]

Reformers and liberals, on the other hand, grew increasingly angry at what they perceived as the Court's obstructionist attitude toward needed economic changes. Many were convinced that property-conscious justices were deliberately sabotaging the New Deal program in order to safeguard corporate interests. "It is a tragic and ominous commentary on our form of government," labor leader John L. Lewis remarked, "when every decision of the Supreme Court seems designed to fatten capital and starve and destroy labor."[11] Further, liberals charged that the Court was inappropriately frustrating decision making by the political majority. They renewed the Progressive argument that the justices should defer to the judgment of the elective branches of government. By the mid-1930s the Court's protection of economic rights was at the center of an acrimonious debate over the place of the judiciary in American political life. The conservative justices were vilified in highly personal terms.

President Roosevelt was gradually drawn into this controversy. In 1935, following the *Schechter* decision, he derided the Court's "horse and buggy definition of interstate commerce." Roosevelt further declared that the country must decide whether "we are going to restore to the Federal Government the powers which exist in the National government of every other nation in the world to enact and administer laws that have a bearing on and general control over national economic problems."[12] Roosevelt's political hand was immeasurably strengthened by his overwhelming reelection in November 1936. Clearly, a substantial majority of the country supported more vigorous governmental control of economic affairs. Laissez-faire constitutionalism no longer commanded a secure base of political support. The conservative majority of the Supreme Court was virtually isolated. Early in 1937 Roosevelt heightened the pressure on the justices by proposing a bill to enlarge the size of the Supreme Court. Such a move would allow the president to name new justices more sympathetic to his economic position. Dubbed a Court-packing plan, Roosevelt's scheme generated bitter bipartisan opposition.

The Court measure, widely viewed as an attack on judicial independence, died in Congress.

Nonetheless, Roosevelt achieved his objective of shifting the Supreme Court's outlook on the protection of economic and property rights. As a practical matter, it is almost impossible for the judiciary to move against strong currents of public opinion for a prolonged period. Hence, continued defiance of popular will carried the grave risk of a direct confrontation with the president and Congress. Such a contest would certainly have undermined the Supreme Court's authority. Prudence, therefore, dictated a judicial retreat. The political climate, combined with the threat of the Court-packing plan, caused the conservative majority to split. Chief Justice Hughes and Justice Roberts adopted a more tolerant approach toward New Deal policies, joining with the previous dissenters to form a new majority favorable to federal and state economic controls. In the process, the Supreme Court undertook a wholesale reversal of landmark decisions. This abrupt change in the Court's thinking, known as the constitutional revolution of 1937, is best understood in the larger political context.

The Supreme Court now moved rapidly away from laissez-faire constitutionalism. In *West Coast Hotel Co. v. Parrish* (1937) the justices sustained a Washington State minimum wage law for women and minors. Speaking for a five-to-four majority, Chief Justice Hughes overruled the *Adkins* precedent and effectively repudiated the liberty of contract doctrine. Decrying the "exploitation of a class of workers who are in an unequal position with respect to bargaining power," he recognized a wide discretion in state legislatures to safeguard employee health and safety and to ensure "freedom from oppression."[13] In dissent, Justice Sutherland asserted that the minimum wage law not only arbitrarily interfered with the right to bargain over wages but also represented discrimination against women by curtailing their ability to compete with men for jobs. The decision in *West Coast Hotel* marked the virtual end of economic due process as a constitutional norm. Since 1937 the Supreme Court has not overturned any economic or social legislation on due process grounds.

At the same time, the Supreme Court dramatically expanded congressional authority over business and commercial activity. Consistent with the New Deal preference for national economic programs, the justices adopted a broad interpretation of the commerce clause. In *NLRB v. Jones & Laughlin Steel Corp.* (1937) the Court heard a challenge to the National Labor Relations Act. This law was the first comprehensive regulation of labor relations. It facilitated the formation of unions and required employers to engage in collective bargaining. As discussed earlier, the Supreme Court had long maintained a definite line between production and commerce. Consequently, the steel company argued that the act was unconstitutionally applied to labor relations in industrial plants. By a five-to-four margin, however, the justices ruled that Congress could regulate activities that directly or indirectly affected interstate commerce. Stressing the close relationship between manufacturing and commerce, the Court reasoned that industrial strife might have a serious impact on interstate commerce. Dissenting, Justice McReynolds lamented the sweeping nature of the decision: "Almost anything— marriage, births, death—may in some fashion affect commerce."[14] Indeed, subsequent cases held that even small businesses with negligible impact on interstate commerce were subject to the National Labor Relations Act.

Changes in the composition of the Supreme Court strengthened the precarious majority supporting the New Deal. Starting in 1937 the remaining conservative justices began to retire. In their place President Roosevelt named such ardent New Dealers as Hugo Black, Stanley Reed, and Felix Frankfurter. By 1940 the reconstituted Supreme Court was solidly under the control of liberal justices.

Over the next few years the Court repeatedly upheld the power of the federal government to oversee economic activity, no matter how negligible the effect was on interstate commerce. In *United States v. Darby* (1941), for instance, the justices unanimously sustained the Fair Labor Standards Act, which fixed the minimum wages and maximum number of hours for employees engaged in producing goods for interstate commerce. The act also prevented the shipment in interstate commerce of goods manufactured in violation of these wage and hour requirements. Speaking for the Court, Justice Harlan Fiske Stone affirmed federal authority over labor relations and production. Validating the prohibition on the movement of goods, he overruled *Hammer v. Dagenhart* (1918) and declared that the Court would not investigate the motive behind regulations of commerce. Stone further concluded that the power of Congress extended to intrastate activities that affected interstate commerce. By deciding that the Tenth Amendment stated "but a truism," Stone removed that provision as a limit on the federal regulation of commerce.[15]

The Supreme Court also approved federal regulation of agricultural production. New Dealers hoped to increase crop prices by restricting the supply. In *Mulford v. Smith* (1939) the justices affirmed the second Agricultural Adjustment Act, which provided for the imposition of marketing quotas on farmers to reduce the volume of crops. The Court went a step further in *Wickard v. Filburn* (1942) and upheld federal power to set quotas for wheat consumed by a farmer for livestock feed and household food on his own land. Justice Robert H. Jackson, writing for the Court, defined congressional authority under the commerce clause in sweeping terms, rejecting the distinction between direct and indirect effect on interstate commerce. Jackson reasoned that the cumulative effect of consumption of a small amount of homegrown wheat by many farmers could have a substantial influence on the market price of wheat.

For all practical purposes, the Supreme Court recognized an unqualified power in Congress to reach any economic activity under the commerce clause. Indeed, the justices stated in 1946 that federal commerce power was "as broad as the economic needs of the nation."[16] The concept of intrastate commerce thus was drained of any substance. To New Dealers this transformation of the commerce clause reflected a realistic assessment of the interdependent character of the national economy and the need for federal control of multistate commercial enterprises. It was difficult, however, to square plenary congressional authority over all commerce with the basic constitutional notion of a limited federal government of enumerated powers. By eliminating the traditional limitations on the exercise of federal commerce power, the Supreme Court opened the door for the rise of the regulatory state. As a result, Congress enacted increasingly intrusive controls over private property and business activity.

In addition to extending the scope of affirmative congressional power under the commerce clause, the Supreme Court heard challenges to numerous state laws as impermissible burdens on interstate commerce. After 1937 the justices were usually sympathetic to state economic regulations, despite an incidental impact on interstate commerce. Thus, in *South Carolina Highway Department v. Barnwell Brothers* (1938) the

Court sustained nondiscriminatory legislation limiting the weight and width of vehicles moving in interstate commerce on state highways. Such restriction was deemed a reasonable police power regulation to protect safety and prevent undue wear and tear on roadways. Likewise, the justices, by a seven-to-two vote, upheld the application of a Pennsylvania law imposing a license requirement on milk dealers to a dealer that shipped all of its milk to another state. In *Milk Control Board v. Eisenberg Farm Products* (1939) the Court upheld the statute as a valid use of the state police power to regulate the production of milk.

When states placed a barrier to the movement of goods or persons across state lines, however, the Supreme Court found such restrictions to constitute an unconstitutional interference with interstate commerce. At issue in *Edwards v. California* (1941) was a statute making it a crime for an individual to bring into California "any indigent person." The state defended the measure by arguing that the huge influx of migrants to California had created serious public health and financial problems. Unanimously rejecting this contention, the Supreme Court emphasized that the transportation of persons was a form of interstate commerce. The justices declared that one state could not "isolate itself from difficulties common to all of them by restraining the transportation of persons and property across its borders."[17] In *Edwards* the Court employed dormant commerce power to achieve a libertarian result.

The New Deal judicial revolution also had important implications for governmental regulation of utility rates. In *Federal Power Commission v. Hope Natural Gas Company* (1944) the Supreme Court abandoned the fair-value standard of *Smyth v. Ames* (1898), ruling that rate-making bodies were not bound to follow any single formula for determining charges. Judicial inquiry was directed only to the impact of the rate order on the regulated industry, not the method of rate calculation. Although utilities were still constitutionally protected against rates set at a confiscatory level, *Hope Natural Gas* allowed the states wide discretion to balance the interests of investors and consumers in setting reasonable utility charges. Speaking for the Court, Justice William O. Douglas broadly affirmed the validity of legal curbs on the rights of property owners. "The fixing of prices, like other applications of the police power," he wrote, "may reduce the value of the property which is being regulated. But the fact that the value is reduced does not mean that the regulation is invalid."[18]

The Supreme Court also strengthened federal power over the economy by adopting a more generous attitude toward the delegation of legislative authority to officials in the executive branch. Moving away from the *Schechter Poultry* precedent, the justices sustained legislation that only set the basic policy and afforded wide latitude to administrators to implement such a policy. This trend reached a high point during World War II when Congress sought to stabilize prices and halt speculation by mandating extensive price and rent controls. In the Emergency Price Control Act of 1942, Congress conferred extensive powers on the Office of Price Administration to fix prices of commodities "which will be generally fair and equitable." The act was challenged on grounds that Congress unconstitutionally delegated its price-fixing power without providing any meaningful standards for the exercise of such authority. In *Yakus v. United States* (1944), however, the Supreme Court upheld the price-fixing scheme. Only Justice Roberts, in dissent, felt that the act prescribed no adequate guidance for the administrators and was therefore invalid. Similarly, the Court, in a companion case, affirmed the act's rent control provisions. The net effect of these decisions was to validate broad administrative controls over enterprises and the use of private property.

Besides a resort to federal and state regulatory authority, the leaders of the New Deal made far-reaching changes in the use of the taxing power. They envisioned individual income taxation as both a financing device and a means of redistributing wealth. During the 1930s additional revenue was necessary to finance the government's growing operations. Congress, for instance, created a host of new regulatory agencies and granted large agricultural subsidies. Further, liberals felt that the wealthy should be taxed more heavily in order to encourage a wider distribution of wealth. Reflecting this sentiment, in the spring of 1935 President Roosevelt complained that the revenue laws "have done little to prevent an unjust concentration of wealth and economic power."[19] Roosevelt's specific tax proposals were less radical than his rhetoric suggested, but he clearly endorsed the principle that government should limit accumulations of great wealth by a few individuals. Critics assailed the president's program as class legislation and confiscatory taxation. Congress warily responded by increasing the tax rates for a relative handful of very rich persons but declined to enlarge the income tax base to encompass middle-class families. Notwithstanding the fear of confiscatory taxes, the redistributive effect of the New Deal tax laws was modest. There was little change during the 1930s in the share of income received by the wealthy. Not until World War II were middle-class households subjected to the federal levy on income.

Another New Deal innovation was the use of federal taxing power for social welfare purposes. The Social Security Act of 1935 imposed a special tax on employers and employees for the payment of benefits for the aged. This provision was attacked on grounds that such an expenditure of federal money was outside the delegated powers of Congress. Adopting a liberal view of the taxing power, the Supreme Court in *Helvering v. Davis* (1937) expansively ruled that Congress could spend money for the general welfare. Moreover, the justices declared that Congress possessed the authority to decide what expenditures were conducive to the general welfare. In effect, the Court sanctioned a comprehensive power in Congress to levy taxes for any purposes that were thought to benefit the public.

This enlarged use of the taxing power during the New Deal carried significant implications for property ownership. The egalitarian premises behind progressive tax rates, coupled with the elimination of constitutional limits on the power to raise taxes, contained an implicit threat to the security of private property. Enhanced tax revenue was unquestionably necessary to finance the operations of modern government. But the existence of an unbridled tax power suggested that property ownership existed merely at the sufferance of Congress. In theory Congress could effectively confiscate property through taxation.

The lacerating struggle over the validity of the New Deal program engendered lasting hostility to the judicial protection of property rights and had a profound impact on the course of American constitutional history. Once the Supreme Court accepted the New Deal, the justices abruptly withdrew from the field of economic regulation. This reflected a monumental change in the Court's attitude toward property rights and entrepreneurial liberty. From its inception, one scholar noted, ''the Court deemed its mission to be the protection of property against depredations by the people and their legislatures. After 1937 it gave up this mission.''[20] A sharply limited concept of property rights thus operated for the next generation.

The cornerstone of this new constitutional direction was a judicially created dichotomy between property rights and personal liberties. This distinction was forcefully articulated by Justice Stone in the famous footnote 4 in *United States v. Carolene Products Co.* (1938). The case arose out of the dairy industry's long campaign against filled milk, a type of evaporated skimmed milk. In 1923 Congress passed the Filled Milk Act, which prohibited the sale of filled milk in interstate commerce. As further evidence of the retreat from economic due process, the Supreme Court upheld the statute, despite its special-interest character and anti-competitive effect. A plurality of the justices accepted at face value the legislative declaration that filled milk was injurious to health. In wide-ranging language the Court stated that the existence of a factual basis supporting economic legislation would be presumed. Henceforth, economic regulations would be found to violate the due process clause only when such legislation did not rest "upon some rational basis within the knowledge and experience of the legislators."[21] Justice Stone added in footnote 4, however, that this presumption of constitutionality had a narrower application to legislation impinging on specific provisions of the Bill of Rights.

By separating property rights from individual freedom, the *Carolene Products* analysis instituted a double standard of constitutional review under which the Supreme Court afforded a higher level of judicial protection to the preferred category of personal rights. Economic rights were implicitly assigned a secondary constitutional status. Because the reasonableness of economic regulations was presumed, judicial scrutiny of legislation under the rational basis test became purely nominal. Consequently, the Court gave great latitude to Congress and state legislatures to fashion economic policy, while expressing only perfunctory concern for the rights of individual property owners. After 1937, as demonstrated in *Carolene Products,* the justices routinely accepted legislative statements of policy, no matter how implausible, as a basis for upholding regulatory measures. A product of the value preferences of the depression era, the decision in *Carolene Products* well illustrated the scant regard for economic rights shown by the emerging liberal constitutionalism. In contrast with the limited role of government under the laissez-faire philosophy, the doctrine of liberal constitutionalism affirmed governmental power to redress social ills, resolve conflicts, regulate business, and intervene in the economy.

Judged from a historical perspective, the theory underlying *Carolene Products* was problematic. The fundamental constitutional dilemma, of course, is that the framers of the Constitution assigned a much higher standing to property ownership than did the New Deal liberals. The distinction between property rights and personal liberties runs counter to the framers' belief that rights are closely related and that the protection of property ownership is essential to the enjoyment of political liberty. In keeping with this ideal, the Constitution does not divide rights into categories. As a practical matter, a line between economic rights and other liberties cannot be drawn with precision. Moreover, it is difficult to reconcile the subordination of property rights with the specific property guarantees in the Constitution. Another problem is that *Carolene Products* simply ignored the Supreme Court's long heritage of safeguarding property ownership from legislative intrusion. Despite some continuing criticism, however, the constitutional double standard in *Carolene Products* quickly became the new orthodoxy.

In the half-century since the constitutional revolution of 1937, property rights have received little substantive protection under the Constitution. The triumph of the New Deal and liberal constitutionalism inaugurated a period in which lawmakers largely exercised free sway in the economic area. Legislation that interfered with the operation of the free market and adjusted the economic interests of groups was regularly sustained. Preoccupied with civil liberties and civil rights, the Supreme Court devoted little time to cases involving property issues. Such developments lend credence to one scholar's conclusion that in the face of expanding economic controls, "property rights were essentially confined to a legal dust bin."[22] But long-standing concepts of economic liberty could not be easily banished from the American constitutional tradition. After World War II, as the sense of economic crisis ebbed, the Supreme Court gingerly returned to the defense of property rights.

8

Property Rights and the Regulatory State

Following World War II, American society experienced a dynamic era of economic growth, rapid technological innovation, and social change. Despite pockets of poverty, most Americans experienced a steadily rising standard of living. Businesses adjusted to the regulatory regime and prospered. Although sharp differences remained concerning the precise role of the government in managing the economy and controlling the usage of private property, few urged a return to the largely unregulated free market before the New Deal. The dominant political ideology supported the regulatory state and looked for a governmental solution to economic ills. Many regulations went far beyond the traditional health and safety rationale and placed costly burdens on property owners. For instance, the drive to secure equal rights for racial minorities and the campaigns for environmental and consumer protection generated a host of new laws that further restricted the use of property and economic liberty. The federal and state governments mushroomed steadily in size and played a large role in nearly every aspect of the economy. As the network of economic regulations grew more intrusive, there was an erosion of individual property rights. Some commentators even suggested that the basic notion of private property ownership had disintegrated.

The growth of government affected property rights in other ways. Federal and state governments offered an increasingly wide range of services and benefits. Through contracts, licenses, public employment, and welfare entitlements government itself soon became a major source of wealth. This prompted a sharp debate over the extent to which these economic interests should receive judicial protection. The increased governmental operations, moreover, generated an enormous need for revenue. Tax policy, with obvious implications for the security of property, became a persistent issue.

In the 1950s and 1960s the Supreme Court, under the leadership of Chief Justice Earl Warren, embraced the jurisprudence of substantive liberalism. Striving to achieve egalitarian goals, the justices sanctioned the growing welfare state and consistently deferred to legislative bodies with respect to economic and social issues. The Court accepted at face value the ostensible legislative objectives in regulation cases. In this climate, the security of property and contractual rights, long a primary function of the federal judiciary, received scant attention. Heavily influenced by New Deal constitutionalism, the Court virtually eliminated property rights from the constitutional agenda for several decades.

Despite this marked shift in attitude, however, judicial concern for the protection of economic rights never entirely disappeared. Thus, the justices continued to oversee the economic regulations of administrative agencies and to protect interstate business against burdensome state regulations. By 1970, national political and intellectual currents had turned in a more conservative direction. Critics questioned the efficacy of regulatory schemes and challenged the New Deal constitutional orthodoxy. A more conservative Supreme Court gradually began to revitalize constitutional protection of economic rights and to invalidate excessive regulations.

The growth of the national government was encouraged by the Supreme Court's expansive interpretation of the commerce clause. After the New Deal the Court found almost all economic activity to be part of interstate commerce and therefore subject to regulation by Congress. In addition, Congress utilized its broad power over commerce to advance noneconomic goals. In 1964, Congress, as a part of a comprehensive civil rights act, prohibited racial discrimination in privately owned places of public accommodation. Fearing that its enforcement power under Section 5 of the Fourteenth Amendment did not reach purely private conduct, Congress enacted the Civil Rights Act on the basis of its commerce power. The Supreme Court in *Katzenbach v. McClung* (1964) sustained the measure as applied to a small family-owned restaurant that catered largely to local patrons. Practically speaking, the power of Congress to control commerce appeared to be boundless.

More than a decade later the Supreme Court, under the influence of more conservative justices, made an abortive attempt to revive state sovereignty as a limitation on federal commerce power. In *National League of Cities v. Usery* (1976), for the first time since the New Deal, the justices, by a five-to-four vote, invalidated a federal statute because it exceeded the scope of the commerce clause. The Court concluded that an attempt by Congress to prescribe minimum wages and maximum hours for state government employees unconstitutionally displaced state authority. A decade later, however, the justices overruled *Usery* and determined that state sovereignty imposes no constitutional restriction on federal commerce power.

By abandoning economic due process, the Supreme Court enhanced the authority of the states to regulate business activity. Yet in an interdependent national economy, state regulations inflicted costs on the consumers of goods in interstate commerce. Companies with multistate operations faced the expensive prospect of complying with inconsistent state laws. Further, state economic legislation often sought to insulate local interests from interstate competition. But such laws threatened to balkanize the national market and to conflict with congressional power under the commerce clause.

As previously discussed, the Court has long adhered to the view that the commerce clause, by its own force, forbids state regulations that interfere with interstate trade. Without congressional legislation, the Court has acted as the arbiter of competing national and state interests. Although the justices have found it difficult to articulate principles that govern the application of this dormant commerce power, they have consistently looked with disfavor on state statutes that discriminate against interstate commerce in favor of local interests or that contradict paramount national legislation. Moreover, the justices have tended to strike down state regulations placing undue burdens on the flow of commerce from state to state. Since World War II the Supreme Court has been repeatedly called on to determine which state regulations may be constitutionally applied to interstate business enterprises.

State safety regulations affecting interstate railroads and trucking have been the source of much controversy. At issue in the landmark case of *Southern Pacific Co. v. Arizona* (1945) was a state law that prohibited the operation of a passenger train of more than fourteen cars or a freight train of more than seventy cars. The state defended the statute as a safety measure to reduce the number of accidents on long trains. Weighing the safety considerations against the economic burden on the railroad, the Supreme Court stressed that the train law impaired transportation efficiency and impeded the interstate movement of long trains. The justices also found only a tenuous connection between the law and the alleged safety concerns. Accordingly, the Court held that the regulation of train lengths went "too far" and contravened the commerce clause. Justice Hugo L. Black, dissenting, accused the majority of substituting its judgment about sound economic policy for that of the state legislature in a manner suggestive of economic due process.

In a line of cases the Supreme Court ruled that state attempts to retain business or preserve economic opportunities for residents could not be achieved by isolating the state from the national economy. South Carolina enacted several laws to restrict nonresidents from commercial shrimp fishing in the state's coastal waters. One measure required all shrimp fishers to dock at South Carolina ports and unload and package their catch. This provision materially increased the operating costs for Georgia shrimpers and thus tended to divert business to South Carolina. In *Toomer v. Witsell* (1948) the Court struck down the docking requirement as an impermissible burden on interstate commerce in shrimp.

During the 1970s and 1980s the Supreme Court became increasingly vigorous in scrutinizing state economic regulations under the dormant commerce power. The Court struck down numerous state statutes restricting the export of goods or giving state residents preferred access to natural resources. For instance, the justices voided an Arizona law requiring that cantaloupes be packaged in the state, an Oklahoma measure curtailing the export of minnows, and an Alaska statute providing that timber taken from state lands be processed within the jurisdiction. Furthermore, the Supreme Court invalidated state statutes that erected discriminatory barriers to the movement of interstate trade. In *City of Philadelphia v. New Jersey* (1978) the Court, by a seven-to-two margin, held that a New Jersey law prohibiting the importation of waste materials was protectionist in nature and therefore impermissible under the commerce clause. Likewise, the Supreme Court ruled in a series of cases that state price affirmation laws for beer and alcoholic beverages violated the commerce clause. The Court reasoned that such measures had the practical effect of controlling commercial activity outside the state and discriminated against interstate beer shippers.

Although the Supreme Court closely examined state economic regulations under the dormant commerce power, the justices sustained measures that had only an incidental impact on commerce or that advanced a strong local interest. By the mid-1980s, corporate takeover bids had become a feature of national economic life. Fearful of an adverse local impact, several states enacted statutes designed to restrict the outside takeover of state-chartered corporations by regulating stock tender offers and making bids more costly. Noting that corporations were governed by state law, the Supreme Court in *CTS Corp. v. Dynamics Corporation of America* (1987) upheld Indiana's antitakeover law by a six to three vote. Speaking for the Court, Justice Lewis F. Powell, Jr., concluded that the act placed only a slight burden on interstate commerce and was justified by the state's interests in protecting shareholders. As a result, states can participate to a significant degree in the regulation of the national securities market. In dissent, Justice Byron R. White argued that the antitakeover law restricted the sale of stock in interstate commerce and represented the type of economic protectionism forbidden by the commerce clause.

Despite some doctrinal confusion, the primary purpose of dormant commerce jurisprudence is to foster free trade within a national marketplace. Judicial opinions speak in terms of safeguarding interstate trade, but in actuality dormant commerce power protects the entrepreneurial liberty of individuals and corporations to conduct business across state lines. In the modern era, judicial review of state economic regulations under the commerce clause serves some of the same functions as economic due process before the constitutional revolution of 1937. By balancing economic interests against a state's rationale for regulation, the Supreme Court effectively inquires into the reasonableness of economic legislation. Thus, dormant commerce jurisdiction preserves an important role for the federal courts in the field of economic rights.

In marked contrast with the Supreme Court's forceful invocation of dormant commerce jurisdiction, the justices have shown no inclination to revive the doctrine of economic due process as a means of safeguarding property rights. The Court has remained highly deferential to legislative decision making and has sustained all economic regulations against due process challenge. In 1949 Justice Black declared that "the due process clause is no longer to be so broadly construed that Congress and state legislatures are put in a straight jacket when they attempt to suppress business and industrial conditions which they regard as offensive to the public welfare."[1] Although the Court occasionally observed that there were limits to legislative power over property rights, no statute was ever found to exceed the scope of regulatory authority. On the contrary, the Court repeatedly stressed the wide power of lawmakers to control business practices.

The abandonment of economic due process culminated in *Williamson v. Lee Optical Co.* (1955). At issue was an Oklahoma law that prevented an optician from fitting or duplicating eyeglass lenses into new frames without a prescription. On its face the measure appeared to be vintage special-interest legislature that burdened consumers and arbitrarily hampered the optician's business. Conceding that the law "may exact a needless, wasteful requirement in many cases," Justice William O. Douglas nonetheless rejected an attack based on the due process clause. Rather than relying on legislative findings to defend the statute, Douglas hypothesized various rationales that "might have" guided the legislature. "It is enough," he concluded, "that there is an evil at hand for correction, and that it might be thought that the particular legislative measure was a rational way to correct it."[2] Justice Douglas suggested that those aggrieved by the law seek political rather than judicial relief. In effect, a state was no longer required to present even a minimal justification for economic regulations. Because virtually any legislation would satisfy the lenient *Lee Optical* standard, judicial review of economic matters under the due process clause was seemingly at an end.

The justices' determination to reject economic due process was also evident in *Ferguson v. Skrupa* (1963). A Kansas statute outlawed the business of debt adjustment except as incident to the practice of law. Skrupa argued that the law prohibited a legitimate activity and thus constituted a violation of his due process rights to conduct a useful business. Writing for the Court, Justice Black abruptly dismissed the due process challenge. Asserting that the Court had returned "to the original constitutional proposition that courts do not substitute their social and economic beliefs for the judgment of legislative bodies," he insisted that the due process clause imposed no limit on state regulation of business.[3]

Changes in the intellectual and political climate gradually undermined the hegemony of New Deal jurisprudence. Even during the heyday of post–New Deal liberalism, some jurists criticized the subordination of property rights. In 1958 Learned Hand, a prominent federal circuit court judge, questioned whether there was a principled distinction between personal and property rights. He observed that "it would have seemed a strange anomaly" to the framers of the Fifth Amendment "to learn that they constituted severer restrictions as to Liberty than Property." Hand added that there was "no constitutional basis" for asserting greater judicial supervision over personal freedom than over economic liberty.[4]

Speaking for the Supreme Court, Justice Potter Stewart amplified this view in *Lynch v. Household Finance Corp.* (1972). Stewart declared "that the dichotomy between personal liberties and property rights is a false one. Property does not have rights. People have rights." In language evoking the attitudes of the framers, he further stated: "In fact, a fundamental interdependence exists between the personal right to liberty and the personal right in property. Neither could have meaning without the other. That rights in property are basic civil rights has long been recognized."[5] Stewart's linkage of property rights with individual liberty contradicted a major tenet of New Deal constitutionalism, which placed economic interests in a separate category deserving less rigorous judicial protection. This approach indicates that the modern Supreme Court is not entirely comfortable with the notion that sharp lines can be drawn between personal and property rights. At the same time, the justices have made no move to reconsider the double standard of judicial review established in *Carolene Products.*

New trends in economic thought also challenged the dominant liberal legal culture. In the 1970s a group of conservative scholars associated with the law and economics and public-choice movements launched a sustained attack on the welfare state and New Deal constitutionalism. Asserting the desirability of the free market, they took a stark view of governmental intervention in the economy. Stressing the importance of efficiency and cost–benefit analysis, these scholars maintained that legal rules should mimic competitive outcomes and thus supplement rather than supplant the free market.[6] They fashioned the theory of rent seeking to describe the capture of the legislative process by organizations or businesses seeking to gain a preferred position in the market at the expense of rivals. Rent-seeking behavior encompasses laws that promote de facto monopolies by restricting business competition, as well as governmental programs designed to transfer wealth from disfavored to

favored groups. To some conservative scholars, such legislation represented both unsound economic policy and an unconstitutional infringement of property rights.

Conservative scholarship also questioned the liberals' faith in a political resolution of economic issues. They charged that well-organized
special-interest groups dominated legislatures and were in the best
position to win rent-seeking favors from lawmakers. Consumers and
small enterprises hurt by economic regulations in fact had no meaningful
access to the political process. Hence, conservatives were skeptical about
the ability of legislative bodies to defend property rights or to protect the
public interest in a free-market economy. Furthermore, they insisted that
the stated purpose of legislation should not be accepted at face value,
because measures ostensibly enacted to protect health, safety, or welfare
often advanced class or special interests.

Influenced by this ideology, several scholars urged the federal courts to
undo the constitutional revolution of 1937 and resume broad judicial
supervision of economic matters. They sought to revive laissez-faire
constitutionalism as a means to defend the free market and prevent
governmental transfers of private wealth. Professor Richard A. Epstein
has asserted that judges "should protect individual liberty and private
property save where the state offers full compensation for the restrictions
it so imposes."[7] These doctrines have stirred up a sharp controversy, and
their impact on judicial decision making remains unclear. Nonetheless,
the new conservative ideology has been an important catalyst in reopening public dialogue about the constitutional protection of economic
rights.

More important, by the late 1960s the political ascendancy of the New
Deal had disintegrated. Weary after years of social upheaval and expensive government programs, the nation took a conservative political turn.
The election of Richard M. Nixon as president in 1968 initiated an era in
which the Republicans again dominated national elections. For the first
time since the 1930s the role of the Supreme Court became a major
campaign issue. Although economic rights were not a source of controversy in 1968, Nixon campaigned vigorously against the liberal activism
of the Warren Court, promising to nominate conservative justices who
would favor "strict construction" of the Constitution. Despite setbacks,
Nixon succeeded in naming four justices and moving the Supreme Court
in a rightward direction in several areas of law.

The sweeping 1980 election victory of President Ronald Reagan, popularly termed the "Reagan revolution," was a significant step in the revival of property rights. Hostile to the regulatory state, Reagan viewed big government as a problem, not a solution. Accordingly, he attempted to curb the scope of governmental activities. Preferring to rely on competition and private economic ordering, Reagan encouraged the partial deregulation of several industries. His economic policy stressed opportunity and growth, downplaying egalitarian objectives. He made substantial cuts in social welfare programs and engineered an income tax reduction that dropped the tax rate for upper-income individuals. With these steps the administration sought to encourage private investment and enterprise rather than to redistribute wealth through taxation. Reagan certainly did not dismantle the regulatory state, but his policies reflected a deep popular commitment to the free-market ideal. In addition, anxious to restrain judicial activism, the Reagan administration invoked the intention of the framers of the Constitution as the legitimate basis for constitutional interpretation. This reliance on the original-intent doctrine left unsettled the appropriate role for the federal judiciary in safeguarding economic liberty.

Reagan also pursued a conservative course in his judicial selection process. The president carefully picked appointees for the federal bench who shared his philosophy of judicial restraint and his skepticism toward governmental regulation. In 1986 Reagan elevated William H. Rehnquist, then the Court's most forceful conservative, to the post of chief justice. Reagan was generally successful in reorienting the direction of the Supreme Court. Several of the Reagan-appointed justices, notably Antonin Scalia, were receptive to the protection of property rights. Moreover, Reagan named several prominent scholars associated with the law and economics movement, such as Richard A. Posner, Frank H. Easterbrook, and Ralph K. Winter, to important positions on the lower federal courts.

These changes in the intellectual and political climate set the stage for a reconsideration of economic liberty within the constitutional scheme. To be sure, the Supreme Court continued to permit Congress and the states wide latitude to impose economic regulations. Occasionally, however, the justices evidenced a less deferential attitude and afforded greater weight to contractual and property rights.

This shift became apparent in the late 1970s when the Supreme Court reinvigorated the long-neglected contract clause. In *United States Trust Co. v. New Jersey* (1977) the justices, for the first time in nearly forty years, applied the clause to strike down a state law. The case arose when New Jersey abrogated a statutory bond covenant prohibiting the use of revenues securing state bonds for mass transit purposes. Speaking for a four-to-three majority of the Court, Justice Harry S. Blackmun stressed that prior decisions did not indicate "that the Contract Clause was without meaning in modern constitutional jurisprudence, or that its limitation on state power was illusory." Justice Blackmun, however, refused to treat the contract clause as an absolute bar to the modification of obligations, and was prepared to accept a reasonable impairment "necessary to serve an important public purpose."[8] He then ruled that more stringent judicial scrutiny was appropriate when states allegedly infringed on their own obligations and found that the repeal of the covenant unreasonably diminished the security of the bondholders. Even this modest revival of the contract clause prompted a heated dissent by Justice William Brennan. He charged that "by creating a constitutional safe haven for property rights embodied in a contract," the decision frustrated legislative policymaking and distorted "modern constitutional jurisprudence governing regulation of private economic interests."[9]

One year later, in *Allied Structural Steel Co. v. Spannaus* (1978) the Supreme Court, by a five-to-three vote, relied on the contract clause to void state infringement of a private contractual arrangement. A Minnesota law retroactively modified the obligations of a company under its pension plan. Declaring that the contract clause "is not a dead letter," Justice Potter Stewart insisted that for the clause to retain any meaning, "it must be understood to impose *some* limits upon the power of a State to abridge existing contractual relationships, even in the exercise of its otherwise legitimate police power."[10] He concluded that the Minnesota legislature had imposed additional financial burdens on the company in contravention of the contract clause. Justice Brennan, again in dissent, urged a narrow interpretation of the clause. He warned that the Court was undermining the modern jurisprudence of property rights that "recognized a broad latitude in States to effect even severe interference with existing economic values when reasonably necessary to promote the general welfare."[11]

These decisions raised the prospect of a muscular contract clause, but in the 1980s the Supreme Court seemingly reverted to a more permissive attitude. In *Energy Reserves Group v. Kansas Power & Light Company* (1983), for instance, the justices unanimously upheld a Kansas law that imposed a ceiling on the contract right of natural gas suppliers to increase prices. Likewise, in *Keystone Bituminous Coal Association v. De-Benedictis* (1987) the Court rejected a contract clause challenge to a Pennsylvania law preventing the enforcement of contractual waivers of liability for surface damage caused by mining. Speaking for a five-to-four majority, Justice John Paul Stevens observed that "the prohibition against impairing the obligation of contracts is not to be read literally."[12] He determined that the state's strong interest in regulating mining practices justified the impairment of private contracts.

The upshot of these seemingly inconsistent decisions is that the contract clause retains a degree of vitality as a safeguard for property rights. Although the modern Supreme Court gives only passing attention to the clause, the justices have invoked it to safeguard existing economic interests against egregious state interference. Several lower federal and state courts also relied on the contract clause during the 1980s to invalidate legislative impairment of private agreements. Oklahoma, Iowa, and Kansas courts, for instance, found state mortgage foreclosure moratorium or redemption statutes to be unconstitutional on this basis.

Because the justices have narrowly construed the contract clause, the takings clause of the Fifth Amendment has emerged as the principal bulwark of property rights in contemporary constitutional law. As Justice Black explained in 1960, the clause "was designed to bar Government from forcing some people alone to bear public burdens which, in all fairness and justice, should be borne by the public as a whole."[13] Spurred first by suburbanization and later by environmental concerns, controls on land use grew progressively more complex after World War II. Both federal and state governments increasingly sought to acquire property for large-scale public projects, such as the interstate highway system, and to restrict owners in the use of their land. Consequently, the Supreme Court has heard numerous cases attacking governmental actions based on the takings clause. In many respects the Court has strengthened public authority over privately owned property but, at the same time, has afforded limited protection to property owners.

The Supreme Court, for all practical purposes, has eliminated the "public use" requirement as a check on the power of government to appropriate private property by means of eminent domain. In the leading case of *Berman v. Parker* (1954) property owners challenged the taking of their land under a comprehensive urban renewal project for redevelopment by a private agency. They contended that property could not be taken from one owner and then resold to another for private use. Rejecting this argument, the Court equated the "public use" clause with the police power. The justices insisted that the "concept of the public welfare is broad and inclusive" and concluded that the judiciary should defer to legislative determinations of the need to use eminent domain.[14] The Court in *Hawaii Housing Authority v. Midkiff* (1984) reaffirmed this policy of judicial deference to the judgment of lawmakers as to what constitutes public use. The justices upheld a Hawaii land reform statute that allowed tenants under long-term leases to acquire by eminent domain the landlord's title to the land. Justice Sandra Day O'Connor, speaking for a unanimous Court, brushed aside the argument that the law simply took the property of one person for transfer to another and ruled that the use of eminent domain need only be "rationally related to a conceivable public purpose."[15] Under this permissive approach several state courts have sustained the public acquisition of land to facilitate industrial development by private corporations.

The Supreme Court has experienced greater difficulty in ascertaining which governmental actions, short of outright seizure, constitute a taking of property for which compensation is mandated. The justices have readily protected landowners against physical intrusion onto their property by the government. In *United States v. Causby* (1946), for instance, regular military flights at low altitude over private land destroyed its value as a farm and invaded the owner's airspace. Reasoning that the land was in effect appropriated, the Court awarded compensation under the takings clause. The justices went a step further in *Loretto v. Teleprompter Manhattan CATV Corp.* (1982), ruling that a New York law requiring the installation of cable television facilities on a landlord's property was a taking for which compensation was due. The Court articulated a rule that any permanent physical occupation of property, no matter how slight, amounted to a taking. Likewise, in other cases the Court found governmental actions eliminating an essential element of property ownership, such as the right to exclude others, to be compensable.

More controversial were regulatory schemes that limited land use. As discussed earlier, the Supreme Court has long recognized that land use controls could have such a severe economic impact as to represent a taking of the property. In practice, however, the justices have been reluctant to invoke the doctrine of regulatory taking and have allowed Congress and the states wide latitude to impose conditions on the use of land. The Court has not established any formula for determining when a restriction of property has gone too far, preferring instead to rely on an ad hoc case-by-case inquiry. Nonetheless, the justices have repeatedly declared that regulations are not unconstitutional simply because they prevent the best use of land or dramatically diminish its value to the owner.

Two decisions illustrate the Supreme Court's deferential approach to land use controls. The Court has allowed cities to enact land use regulations that enhance the aesthetic features of municipal life. In *Penn Central Transportation v. New York* (1978), the Court, by a six-to-three vote, sustained the designation of Grand Central Terminal as a historic landmark, even though such action prevented the landowner from modifying the building in any manner without municipal permission, thereby causing a drastic reduction in its value. Justice William Brennan, speaking for the Court, stressed that the landowner could use the terminal for its original purpose and was able to earn a reasonable return on its investment. In dissent, Justice Rehnquist argued that a taking had occurred and that the costs of a historic preservation program should be borne by taxpayers generally, not individual landowners. In *Agins v. City of Tiburon* (1980) land developers challenged a municipal zoning ordinance restricting construction on a five-acre tract of unimproved land in a desirable suburban area to five single-family residences. The plaintiffs had planned to construct an apartment building on the lot. The Supreme Court rejected the argument that the enactment of the ordinance constituted a taking of property. Writing for the Court, Justice Powell noted that the application of zoning laws effected a taking only "if the ordinance does not substantially advance legitimate state interests . . . or denies an owner economically viable use of his land."[16] He found that the Tiburon ordinance served a legitimate function by preserving open space and ensuring the orderly development of residential property. Powell emphasized, too, that the ordinance did not prohibit use of the land and that the developers were free to submit building plans to local officials.

This generous understanding of regulatory authority has encouraged far-reaching governmental infringement on the traditional rights of

owners to enjoy their property. Such controls often place heavy compliance costs on landowners. Other regulations, such as rent control, are
frankly redistributionist, designed to transfer economic benefits from
property owners to the less advantaged. Many suburban localities used
land use laws to preserve existing amenities and to exclude unwanted
outsiders. Faced with resistance to higher taxes, communities also
resorted to regulation as a means of obtaining services at the expense of
private landowners. Regulatory bodies increasingly conditioned the
granting of building permits to developers upon the dedication of land to
public use or the payment of impact fees to finance other municipal
projects. Such exactions represented a kind of special tax on land
development, a levy which ultimately increased the cost of land to
newcomers. Critics of the regulatory regime charged that the cost of
achieving socially desirable benefits was unfairly placed on landowners
rather than on the general public, in contradiction of the takings clause.

Perhaps dissatisfied with the consequences of its hands-off policy
toward land use controls, in 1987 the Supreme Court took a fresh look
at the question of regulatory taking. As a result, the justices strengthened
the position of property owners against governmental authority to reduce
the value of their property by means of regulation. In the significant case
of *Nollan v. California Coastal Commission* (1987) the Supreme Court,
for the first time since the 1920s, struck down a land use regulation. The
case arose when a state agency conditioned a permit to rebuild a beach
house on the owner's grant of a public easement across the beachfront.
The Court held, by a margin of five-to-four, that the imposition of such a
condition constituted a taking because the requirement was unrelated to
any problem caused by the development. The Court also indicated a
willingness to examine more carefully the connection between the
purpose and the means of regulations. Writing for the Court, Justice
Scalia added: "We view the Fifth Amendment's property clause to be
more than a pleading requirement and compliance with it to be more than
an exercise in cleverness and imagination."[17]

The *Nollan* decision alarmed land use regulators because it signaled a
heightened degree of judicial supervision. Some state and lower federal
courts have begun to take a closer look at regulations placing conditions
on building projects and at rent control programs. In *First English
Evangelical Lutheran Church v. County of Los Angeles* (1987) the
justices ruled, as well, that a property owner may be entitled to compen-

sation for the temporary loss of land use when controls are later invalidated. This decision raised the prospect of damage awards against excessive regulations. In response to these "fundamental changes in takings law," President Reagan issued an executive order in 1988 directing that federal agencies evaluate the effect of their actions "on constitutionally protected property rights" in order to reduce the risk of unlawful regulations.[18]

This resurgent interest in property rights was also manifest in renewed judicial review of utility rate making under the takings clause. After neglecting the area of utility rates since the New Deal era, the Supreme Court cautiously reentered the field in *Duquesne Light Co. v. Barasch* (1989). The justices upheld the Pennsylvania rate order in question and reaffirmed that no particular rate-making method was mandated by the Constitution. Yet the Court emphasized that "the Constitution protects utilities from being limited to a charge for their property serving the public which is so 'unjust' as to be confiscatory."[19] The decision therefore left room for the federal courts to intervene in the state regulatory process by invoking the takings clause.

In addition to the takings clause, the federal courts have occasionally employed the equal protection clause of the Fourteenth Amendment to safeguard economic interests. Generally the states have been accorded broad authority to classify and regulate business activity. In *City of New Orleans v. Dukes* (1976), for example, the Supreme Court upheld a local ordinance prohibiting pushcart food sales but containing a "grandfather" exemption for long-established vendors. More recently, however, the Court has exhibited a willingness to scrutinize economic legislation that singled out one category of property for inequitable treatment. This became evident in *Allegheny Pittsburgh Coal Co. v. Webster County* (1989), a case involving county tax assessments on real property. The justices unanimously ruled that taxes must be evenly applied to comparable properties and that the systematic undervaluation of some property in the same tax class denied other taxpayers equal protection. According to the Court, "the constitutional requirement is the seasonable attainment of a rough equality in tax treatment of similarly situated property owners."[20] This ruling appeared to cast doubt on tax assessment practices in many jurisdictions. During the late 1980s, lower federal courts also found state or local economic regulations to violate the equal protection clause. Courts struck down a utility rate base measure directed against a single company and a municipal ordinance that prohibited a sidewalk shoeshine business.

Traditional property rights sometimes collide with other constitutionally protected rights, requiring the courts to strike a balance between competing values. The right of property owners to maintain exclusive possession of their property has long been deemed an essential element of private property. Yet this right to exclude persons may have the effect of hampering others in the exercise of their constitutional guarantees. In the early 1960s the justices were sympathetic to sit-in demonstrators who protested racial discrimination by remaining on private property. The Supreme Court overturned numerous trespass convictions. More recently, the exclusion of persons who picket or distribute literature in privately owned shopping centers has also generated controversy. In a series of cases during the 1970s the Court affirmed the private nature of property, even when open to the public for commercial purposes. Giving renewed vigor to property rights, the Court held that owners could restrict speech activities on their land. These decisions seemingly favored the prerogatives of private property ownership over the First Amendment guarantee of free speech. Most state courts have likewise ruled that landowners may exclude individuals who engage in such activities.

For a brief period in the 1970s, courts and commentators flirted with the protection of various government benefits as a type of "new property." The basic question was whether social security and welfare benefits and public employment should be viewed as rights or as privileges subject to being withdrawn. Anxious to promote egalitarianism, liberals argued that the judiciary should safeguard welfare recipients and government employees from arbitrary deprivation of their livelihood. This contention was particularly ironic, because since the New Deal era, liberal constitutionalism has offered little protection to traditional forms of property. Critics charged that the "new property" notion was simply a subterfuge to constitutionalize the welfare state and protect the economic interests of political liberals. In *Goldberg v. Kelly* (1970) the justices, by a vote of five-to-four, edged toward acceptance of the new property concept. They held that New York violated due process procedural guarantees by terminating welfare benefits without a prior hearing. Ultimately, however, the Supreme Court declined to treat most entitlements under government programs as traditional property rights for the purpose of due process. Instead, the Court preserved a large measure of legislative authority to manage and even eliminate benefit schemes.

The new property controversy highlighted the conflicting themes surrounding the analysis of property rights. Justice Brennan, a persistent critic of extending constitutional protection to traditional economic interests, was a leader in the move to recognize entitlements and public employment as forms of property. He even echoed the framers by contending that secure economic rights would enable the poor "to participate meaningfully in the life of the community."[21] Brennan thus refurbished the conservative doctrine that respect for property rights secured political freedom to serve egalitarian ends. The conservative justices, on the other hand, rejected the new property theory, adopting the liberal approach that the courts should defer to state control of economic matters.

The quest for racial equality also has significant implications for the allocation of certain economic benefits. During the 1970s, affirmative action became a divisive issue in American society and proved vexing for the Supreme Court as well. Affirmative action programs were grounded on the notion that it was desirable to give preferential treatment to members of racial minorities as compensation for the effects of past discrimination. Congress, as well as state and local governments, adopted preferential hiring for racial minorities or set aside a percentage of public works for minority enterprises. Affirmative action is essentially a means of redistributing economic benefits in the form of governmental employment or contractual opportunities. The difficulty, of course, is that such redistribution in favor of disadvantaged groups inevitably penalized others, prompting challenges under the equal protection clause of the Fourteenth Amendment. On this basis the Reagan administration opposed affirmative action as an invalid racial classification.

Reflecting the uncertainty in society, the Supreme Court in the 1980s equivocated on affirmative action. The justices upheld some affirmative action plans but struck down others when they viewed the justification as not compelling. In *City of Richmond v. J. A. Croson Co.* (1989) the justices, by a six-to-three vote, invalidated a Richmond set-aside program requiring that 30 percent of the dollar amount of municipal construction contracts be awarded to minority enterprises. Justice O'Connor, speaking for the Court, reasoned that the quota plan was not carefully tailored to remedy prior discrimination and thus that it classified citizens on a racial basis in violation of the equal protection clause. The upshot of *Croson* was to curtail the authority of state and local governments to grant economic benefits along racial lines. Although the future of affirmative action is unresolved, the adoption of race-conscious schemes demonstrates that social policies may impinge on the economic interests of individuals.

By 1990 it was apparent that the Supreme Court was continuing to play a major role in safeguarding economic rights. Although there was no evidence that the justices were prepared to resume far-ranging scrutiny of legislation under the doctrine of economic due process, they vigorously protected interstate markets and were less deferential to state laws that infringed on property and contractual rights. Even a modest revival of constitutional safeguards for property ownership threatened the redistributionist goals behind many regulatory programs. Yet, as throughout its history, the Court was simply moving in conformity with the changing political climate.

9

Epilogue

The Constitution and Bill of Rights affirmed the central place of property ownership in American society. Throughout much of American history the Supreme Court has championed property rights against legislative abridgment. In defending property owners, the Supreme Court has reflected not only the views of the framers but also the values deeply embedded in the political culture. From the colonial era to the present, Americans have, with remarkable consistency, assigned a high place to private property and a free-market economy. Widespread property ownership encouraged economic self-sufficiency and political independence. Alexis de Tocqueville, the astute French observer of antebellum society, declared: "In no other country in the world is the love of property keener or more alert than in the United States, and nowhere else does the majority display less inclination toward doctrines which in any way threaten the way property is owned."[1]

This approving attitude toward property ownership continued in the twentieth century. A survey conducted in the late 1970s demonstrated that a large majority of the public believed that private property was as important as freedom to a "good society."[2] As one commentator colorfully asserted: "I can certainly conceive of rational people who, if pressed to a choice, would be willing to give up the right to wear a jacket with obscene words on it in order to retain the right to construct a building or run a railroad."[3]

At the same time, the rise of the modern business corporation transformed thinking about property rights. Although remaining devoted to property ownership, Americans realized that unbridled economic power

153

in private hands was prone to abuses. Gradually moving away from the laissez-faire philosophy, most Americans embraced governmental regulation of business enterprise and land use. Accordingly, lawmakers attempted to curtail monopoly, provide a measure of economic security, safeguard the environment, and regulate labor relations and workplace conditions. Many of these measures, however, restricted traditional property rights. As a result, the Supreme Court long functioned as an arbiter, weighing the needs of the government to regulate economic activity with the right of individuals and corporations to enjoy their property. Following the constitutional revolution of 1937, however, the justices largely abandoned their historic role as a defender of economic rights.

Some commentators believe that the Supreme Court is poised for a significant revival of interest in property rights. Reading the future is always hazardous, but it seems unlikely that the justices will challenge the political branches of government or strike down any major aspect of the regulatory state. Rather, the justices will probably continue on their present course of incrementally extending protection for economic liberty against arbitrary or excessive regulation.

Notwithstanding the central place of property rights in American constitutional history, competing considerations suggest that even an increasingly conservative Supreme Court will move carefully in the economic field. First, some justices, notably Chief Justice William H. Rehnquist, attach a strong value to federalism and support extensive state authority to regulate property. This commitment to federalism often clashes with an enlarged protection of property ownership from state interference.[4] Second, one strain of conservative thought has long favored a reduced role for the federal judiciary in American life. An activist Supreme Court protecting economic interests would be antithetical to this objective. Although the current justices are far more concerned with property rights than their liberal predecessors, these other components of their judicial outlook will constrain the Court's review of economic legislation.

The Supreme Court must carefully adjust the demands of political democracy with the explicit protection of property ownership contained in the Constitution. From an institutional perspective, the Supreme Court cannot afford to be perceived as being overly solicitous of business enterprise and property owners, to the disadvantage of the general public.

Great disparities in wealth and economic power raise the danger of political upheaval and social unrest, which might ultimately threaten private property. Some regulation of existing property rights also is necessary to preserve economic opportunity for others.

Conversely, the facile suggestion in many Court opinions after 1937 that economic questions should be left entirely to the political process is also troubling. If individuals or enterprises have only those property rights that legislators choose to recognize, then property ownership is simply a matter of legislative sufferance. No other important rights are treated in such a cavalier fashion. Lawmakers often seek to benefit segments of society at the expense of property owners. Much legislation frankly seeks to achieve a wider distribution of wealth by divesting owners of their right to use property to its maximum advantage and by altering contractual arrangements. Such opportunistic behavior is less painful to lawmakers than levying taxes to finance governmental programs.

Constitutional protection of economic rights remains important for both utilitarian and libertarian purposes. Property and contractual arrangements constitute the legal foundation of the free-market system. Judicial defense of property ownership enhances private economic ordering and helps secure the investment capital necessary for economic growth. At the same time, recognition of economic rights serves the cause of individual liberty.[5] An economic system resting on private property ownership tends to diffuse political power and to strengthen individual autonomy from governmental control. This relationship between political freedom and a market economy is graphically illustrated by recent developments in Eastern Europe. Almost without exception, the newly independent Eastern European nations have moved to restore private ownership of property and to privatize segments of industry. Even the Soviet Union, the cradle of Marxism, has begun to experiment with marketplace economics.

The Constitution and Bill of Rights, as interpreted by the Supreme Court, have done much to safeguard property ownership, investment capital, the business corporation, and the national market in the face of hostile governmental actions. During the 1990s a more conservative Supreme Court may well revitalize the constitutional protection of economic rights and be somewhat less deferential to legislative interference with the use and enjoyment of property. A return to laissez-faire constitutionalism, however, appears highly problematic. In the last analysis, the viability of property rights, like all individual rights, rests on broad popular acceptance. Thus, the Supreme Court will continue to strike a balance between popular democracy and private property ownership.

Notes

Introduction

1. Felix Frankfurter, *Of Law and Men* (New York: Harcourt Brace, 1956), p. 19.

2. *Chicago, Burlington and Quincy Railroad Company v. Chicago*, 166 U.S. 226, 235 (1897).

3. Thomas C. Gray, "The Malthusian Constitution," 41 *University of Miami Law Review* 21 (1986): 21.

4. James W. Ely, Jr., and David J. Bodenhamer, "Regionalism and American Legal History: The Southern Experience" 39 *Vanderbilt Law Review* 539 (1986): 551–54.

5. James Willard Hurst, *Law and the Conditions of Freedom in the Nineteenth-Century United States* (Madison: University of Wisconsin Press, 1956), p. 24.

6. *Parham v. Justices of Inferior Court of Decatur County*, 9 Ga. 341, 348 (1851).

Chapter 1

1. Willi Paul Adams, *The First American Constitutions: Republican Ideology and the Making of the State Constitutions in the Revolutionary Era* (Chapel Hill: University of North Carolina Press, 1980), p. 191.

2. As quoted in Patricia U. Bonomi, *A Factious People: Politics and Society in Colonial New York* (New York: Columbia University Press, 1971), p. 195.

3. William Penn, *The Excellent Privilege of Liberty and Property Being the Birth-Right of the Free-Born Subjects of England* (1687).

4. Suffolk County Freeholders' Declaration, May 3, 1689, in Michael G.

157

Hall, Lawrence H. Leder, and Michael G. Kammen, eds., *The Glorious Revolution in America* (Chapel Hill: University of North Carolina Press, 1964), p. 103.

5. As quoted in Richard Hofstadter, *America at 1750: A Social Portrait* (New York: Knopf, 1971), p. 140.

6. Dieter Cunz, *The Maryland Germans: A History* (Princeton, N.J.: Princeton University Press, 1948), p. 126.

7. John Locke, *Second Treatise on Government,* in Peter Laslett, ed., *Two Treatises of Government,* 2nd ed. (Cambridge: Cambridge University Press, 1967), p. 380.

8. John Trenchard, Cato's Letters, no. 68, March 3, 1721, in David L. Jacobson, ed., *The English Libertarian Heritage* (Indianapolis: Bobbs-Merrill, 1965), pp. 177–78.

9. William Blackstone, *Commentaries on the Laws of England* (London, 1765, reprinted Chicago: University of Chicago Press, 1979), vol. 1, p. 135.

10. Benjamin Colman, *Some Reasons and Arguments Offered to the Good People of Boston and Adjacent Places for the Setting Up Markets in Boston* (Boston, 1719), p. 8; Boston *Evening Post,* September 12, 1763.

11. Thomas F. DeVoe, *The Market Book: A History of the Public Markets of the City of New York* (New York, 1862, reprinted New York: A. M. Kelley, 1970), p. 147.

12. Blackstone, *Commentaries,* vol. 1, p. 135.

13. William B. Stoebuck, "A General Theory of Eminent Domain," *Washington Law Review,* 47 (1972): 553–79.

Chapter 2

1. Arthur Lee, *An Appeal to the Justice and Interests of the People of Great Britain, in the Present Dispute with America,* 4th ed. (New York, 1775), p. 14.

2. Massachusetts Circular Letter, February 11, 1768, reprinted in Henry Steele Commager, ed., *Documents of American History,* 9th ed. (New York: Appleton–Century–Crofts, 1973), pp. 66–67.

3. Association of Members of the Late House of Burgesses (May 27, 1774), Julian P. Boyd, ed., *The Papers of Thomas Jefferson* (Princeton, N.J.: Princeton University Press, 1950), vol. 1, pp. 107–8.

4. *Votes and Proceedings of the House of Representatives of the Government [of Delaware]* (1765–70) (Wilmington, 1770; reprinted, Dover, Del. for Public Archives Commission, 1931), p. 54.

5. John Phillip Reid, *Constitutional History of the American Revolution: The Authority of Rights* (Madison: University of Wisconsin Press, 1986), p. 27.

6. Edmund Burke, "Speech on Conciliation with America," in *The Works of*

Edmund Burke, 9 vols. (Boston: Charles C. Little and James Brown, 1839), vol. 2, p. 33.

7. Willi Paul Adams, *The First American Constitutions: Republican Ideology and the Making of the State Constitutions in the Revolutionary Era* (Chapel Hill: University of North Carolina Press, 1980), p. 193.

8. Gordon S. Wood, *The Creation of the American Republic, 1776–1787* (Chapel Hill: University of North Carolina Press, 1969), p. 53.

9. *Respublica v. Sparhawk,* 1 Dallas 357, 362 (Pa. 1788).

10. *Cooper v. Telfair,* 4 U.S. 14, 19 (1800).

11. Herbert A. Johnson, "The Palmetto and the Oak: Law and Constitution in Early South Carolina, 1670–1800," in Kermit L. Hall and James W. Ely, Jr., eds., *An Uncertain Tradition: Constitutionalism and the History of the South* (Athens: University of Georgia Press, 1989), p. 98.

12. Notes for Speech Opposing Paper Money (November 1786), in Robert A. Rutland and William M. E. Rachal, eds., *The Papers of James Madison* (Chicago: University of Chicago Press, 1975), vol. 9, p. 158.

13. "Considerations on the Power to Incorporate the Bank of North America," in James DeWitt Andrews, ed., *The Works of James Wilson* (Chicago: Callaghan and Company, 1896), vol. 1, pp. 565–66.

14. Forrest McDonald, *Novus Ordo Seclorum: The Intellectual Origins of the Constitution* (Lawrence: University of Kansas Press, 1985), p. 154.

15. *Brown v. Maryland,* 25 U.S. 419, 446 (1827).

16. John Marshall to James Wilkinson, January 5, 1787, in Herbert A. Johnson, ed., *The Papers of John Marshall, 1775–1788* (Chapel Hill: University of North Carolina Press, 1974), vol. 1, p. 201.

17. Address of the Annapolis Convention, in Harold C. Syrett, ed., *The Papers of Alexander Hamilton, 1782–1786* (New York: Columbia University Press, 1962), vol. 3, pp. 686–89.

18. Adams, *The First American Constitutions,* supra note 7, p. 217, n. 103.

Chapter 3

1. Max Farrand, ed. *The Records of the Federal Convention of 1787,* rev. ed., 5 vols. (New Haven, Conn.: Yale University Press, 1937), vol 1, p. 534.

2. Ibid., p. 302.

3. "Discourses on Davila," in Charles Francis Adams, ed., *The Works of John Adams,* 10 vols. (Boston: Little, Brown, 1851), vol. 6, p. 280. Hereafter cited as *Works of John Adams.*

4. See James W. Ely, Jr., " 'The Good Old Cause': The Ratification of the Constitution and Bill of Rights in South Carolina," in Robert J. Haws, ed., *The*

South's Role in the Creation of the Bill of Rights (Jackson: University Press of Mississippi, 1991).

5. William M. Wiecek, *The Sources of Antislavery Constitutionalism in America, 1760–1848* (Ithaca, N.Y.: Cornell University Press, 1977), p. 63.

6. *Works of John Adams*, p. 280.

7. *The Federalist* (New York: Knickerbocker Press, 1908), p. 205. Hereafter cited as *The Federalist*.

8. Kermit L. Hall, *The Magic Mirror: Law in American History* (New York: Oxford University Press, 1989), p. 69.

9. *The Federalist*, pp. 53–59.

10. Ibid., p. 546.

11. Jonathan Elliot, ed., *The Debates in the Several State Conventions on the Adoption of the Federal Constitution*, 2nd ed., 5 vols. (Philadelphia, 1836–59; reprinted Salem, N.H.: Ayer Company, 1987), vol. 4, pp. 333–36. Hereafter cited as *Debates*.

12. *The Federalist*, p. 279.

13. David Ramsay, *An Address to the Freeman of South Carolina on the Federal Constitution* (Charleston, 1788), in Paul Leicester Ford, ed., *Pamphlets on the Constitution of the United States* (Brooklyn, N.Y., 1888; reprinted 1968), pp. 379–80.

14. Elliot, *Debates*, vol. 4, p. 191.

15. Herbert J. Storing, ed., *The Complete Anti-Federalist*, 7 vols. (Chicago: University of Chicago Press, 1981), vol. 2, p. 64.

16. Elliot, *Debates*, vol. 3, p. 474.

17. Ibid., vol. 4, p. 286.

18. Ibid., vol. 1, p. 322.

19. Edward Dumbauld, *The Bill of Rights and What It Means Today* (Norman: University of Oklahoma Press, 1957), pp. 182–84, 198–200.

20. Elliot, *Debates*, vol. 1, p. 323.

21. Charles F. Hobson and Robert A. Rutland, eds., *The Papers of James Madison* (Charlottesville: University Press of Virginia, 1979), vol. 12, p. 200.

22. "Property," in Robert A. Rutland and Thomas A. Mason, eds., *The Papers of James Madison* (Charlottesville: University Press of Virginia, 1983), vol. 14, pp. 266–68.

23. Charles F. Hobson and Robert A. Rutland, eds., *The Papers of James Madison* (Charlottesville: University Press of Virginia, 1979), vol. 12, pp. 204–7.

24. C. Peter Magrath, *Yazoo: Law and Politics in the New Republic: The Case of Fletcher v. Peck* (Providence, R.I.: Brown University Press, 1966).

25. Harold C. Syrett, ed., *The Papers of Alexander Hamilton* (New York: Columbia University Press, 1973), vol. 19, p. 300.

Chapter 4

1. *Commonwealth v. Alger,* 61 Mass. 53, 85 (1851).

2. *Mayor and Aldermen of Mobile v. Yuille,* 3 Ala. 137, 140 (1841).

3. *Vanhorne's Lessee v. Dorrance,* 2 Dallas 304, 310 (1795).

4. *Calder v. Bull,* 3 Dallas 386, 388 (1798).

5. Leonard W. Levy, *The Law of the Commonwealth and Chief Justice Shaw* (Cambridge, Mass: Harvard University Press, 1957), p. 280.

6. James Willard Hurst, *Law and the Conditions of Freedom in the Nineteenth-Century United States* (Madison: University of Wisconsin Press, 1956), p. 18.

7. *Fletcher v. Peck,* 10 U.S. 87, 137, 139 (1810).

8. *Dartmouth College v. Woodward,* 17 U.S. 518, 644 (1819).

9. *Providence Bank v. Billings,* 29 U.S. 514, 561, 563 (1830).

10. *Charles River Bridge v. Warren Bridge,* 36 U.S. 420, 549, 552–53 (1837).

11. R. Kent Newmyer, *Supreme Court Justice Joseph Story: Statesman of the Old Republic* (Chapel Hill: University of North Carolina Press, 1985), p. 231.

12. *Bronson v. Kinzie,* 42 U.S. 311, 318 (1843).

13. *Gibbons v. Ogden,* 22 U.S. 1, 193, 194, 197 (1824).

14. Charles Warren, *The Supreme Court in United States History,* rev. ed., 2 vols. (Boston: Little, Brown, 1926), vol. 1, p. 616.

15. *Brown v. Maryland,* 25 U.S. 419, 447 (1827).

16. *Willson v. Black Bird Creek Marsh Co.,* 27 U. S. 245, 252 (1829).

17. *Cooley v. Board of Wardens,* 53 U.S. 298, 318 (1852).

18. *Vanhorne's Lessee v. Dorrance,* 2 Dallas 304, 311 (1795).

19. *Calder v. Bull,* 3 Dallas 386, 400 (1798).

20. *West River Bridge Company v. Dix,* 47 U.S. 507, 520 (1848).

21. *Bowman v. Middleton,* 1 Bay 252, 254 (S.C. 1792).

22. *Wynehamer v. People,* 13 N.Y. 378, 399 (1856).

23. *Murray's Lessee v. Hoboken Land and Improvement Co.,* 59 U.S. 272, 276 (1856).

24. James Kent, *Commentaries on American Law* (New York: O. Halsted, 1827), vol. 2, p. 1, 270–76.

25. *Wilkinson v. Leland,* 27 U.S. 627, 657 (1829).

Chapter 5

1. Emancipation Proclamation (1863), U.S. Stat. at L., No. 17, 1268–69.

2. *Slaughterhouse Cases,* 83 U.S. 36, 122 (1873).

3. *Munn v. Illinois,* 94 U.S. 113, 130 (1877).

4. Ibid., p. 140.

5. David N. Mayer, "The Jurisprudence of Christopher G. Tiedeman: A Study in the Failure of Laissez-Faire Constitutionalism," *Missouri Law Review* 55 (1990): 93.

6. Benjamin R. Twiss, *Lawyers and the Constitution: How Laissez Faire Came to the Supreme Court* (Princeton, N.J.: Princeton University Press, 1942).

7. Michael Les Benedict, "Laissez-Faire and Liberty: A Re-Evaluation of the Meaning and Origins of Laissez-Faire Constitutionalism," *Law and History Review* 3 (1985): 293.

8. *Stone v. Farmers' Loan & Trust Co.*, 116 U.S. 307, 331 (1886).

9. See Herbert Hovenkamp, "The Political Economy of Substantive Due Process," *Stanford Law Review* 40 (1988): 379.

10. *Mugler v. Kansas*, 123 U.S. 623, 661 (1887).

11. *Smyth v. Ames*, 169 U.S. 466, 547 (1898).

12. *Allgeyer v. Louisiana*, 165 U.S. 578, 589 (1897).

13. *Lawton v. Steele*, 152 U.S. 133, 137 (1894).

14. *Holden v. Hardy*, 169 U.S. 366, 397 (1898).

15. *Monongahela Navigation Company v. United States*, 148 U.S. 312, 325 (1893).

16. *Mugler v. Kansas*, 123 U.S. 623, 668–69 (1887).

17. Ibid., p. 678.

18. John V. Orth, *The Judicial Power of the United States: The Eleventh Amendment in the Constitution* (New York: Oxford University Press, 1987).

19. *Pensacola Telegraph Company v. Western Union Telegraph Company*, 96 U.S. 1, 9 (1877).

20. *Wabash, St. Louis & Pacific Railway v. Illinois*, 118 U.S. 557, 577 (1886).

21. *United States v. E. C. Knight Co.*, 156 U.S. 1, 12 (1895).

22. For Choates's argument in the *Pollock* cases, see Frederick C. Hicks, ed., *Arguments and Addresses of Joseph Hodges Choate* (St. Paul: West Publishing Company, 1926), pp. 419–526.

23. *Pollock v. Farmers' Loan & Trust Co.*, 157 U.S. 429, 607 (1895).

24. *Pollock v. Farmers' Loan & Trust Co.*, 158 U.S. 601, 695 (1895).

25. Lawrence M. Friedman, *A History of American Law*, 2nd ed. (New York: Simon & Schuster, 1985), p. 567.

Chapter 6

1. For a judicious treatment of the *Lochner* litigation, see Paul Kens, *Judicial Power and Reform Politics: The Anatomy of Lochner v. New York* (Lawrence: University Press of Kansas, 1990).

2. *Lochner v. New York*, 198 U.S. 45, 61 (1905).

3. Ibid., p. 64.

4. Ibid., p. 75.

5. Ibid.

6. *Adkins v. Children's Hospital,* 261 U.S. 525, 546 (1923).

7. *Buchanan v. Warley,* 245 U.S. 60, 74 (1917).

8. *Shreveport Rate Case,* 234 U.S. 342, 351–52 (1914).

9. See, generally, Stephen B. Wood, *Constitutional Politics in the Progressive Era: Child Labor and the Law* (Chicago: University of Chicago Press, 1968).

10. *Hammer v. Dagenhart,* 247 U.S. 251, 276 (1918).

11. *Bailey v. Drexel Furniture Co.,* 259 U.S. 20, 38 (1922).

12. *Pennsylvania Coal Co. v. Mahon,* 260 U.S. 393, 415 (1922).

13. Ibid. For an insightful discussion of this litigation, see Lawrence M. Friedman, "A Search for Seizure: Pennsylvania Coal Co. v. Mahon in Context," *Law and History Review* 4 (1986): 1.

14. *Nectow v. City of Cambridge,* 277 U.S. 183, 188 (1928).

15. *Block v. Hirsh,* 256 U.S. 135, 156 (1921).

16. Ibid., p. 165.

17. Robert M. LaFollette, Introduction to Gilbert E. Roe, *Our Judicial Oligarchy* (New York, 1912), p. v.

18. Charles A. Beard, *An Economic Interpretation of the Constitution of the United States* (New York, 1913). For an attack on the Beard thesis, see Forrest McDonald, *We the People: The Economic Origins of the Constitution* (Chicago: University of Chicago Press, 1958).

Chapter 7

1. *New State Ice Co. v. Liebmann,* 285 U.S. 262, 311 (1932).

2. *Home Building and Loan Association v. Blaisdell,* 290 U.S. 398, 473 (1934).

3. *Nebbia v. New York,* 291 U.S. 502, 537, 527–28 (1934).

4. Ibid., p. 558.

5. *Schechter Poultry Corp. v. United States,* 295 U.S. 495, 529 (1935).

6. *Carter v. Carter Coal Co.,* 298 U.S. 238, 308 (1936).

7. *United States v. Butler,* 297 U.S. 1, 61 (1936).

8. *Louisville Bank v. Radford,* 295 U.S. 555, 602 (1935).

9. Herbert Hoover, "The Confused State of the Union," February 12, 1936, in Herbert Hoover, *Addresses upon the American Road, 1933–1938* (New York: Scribner, 1938), p. 116.

10. As quoted in William H. Harbaugh, *Lawyer's Lawyer: The Life of John W. Davis* (New York: Oxford University Press, 1973), p. 347.

11. As quoted in Drew Pearson and Robert S. Allen, *The Nine Old Men* (Garden City, N.Y.: Doubleday, Doran, 1937), p. 313.

12. *Complete Presidential Press Conferences of Franklin D. Roosevelt* (New York: Da Capo Press, 1972), vol. 5, pp. 315–36.

13. *West Coast Hotel Co. v. Parrish*, 300 U.S. 379, 399 (1937).

14. *National Labor Relations Board v. Jones & Laughlin Steel Corp.*, 301 U.S. 1, 99 (1937).

15. *United States v. Darby*, 312 U.S. 100, 124 (1941).

16. *American Power & Light Co. v. Securities and Exchange Commission*, 329 U.S. 90, 104 (1946).

17. Edwards v. California, 314 U.S. 160, 173 (1942).

18. *Federal Power Commission v. Hope Natural Gas Co.*, 320 U.S. 591, 601 (1944).

19. 79 Cong. Rec. 9657 (1935).

20. Leo Pfeffer, *This Honorable Court: A History of the United States Supreme Court* (Boston: Beacon Press, 1965), p. 322.

21. *United States v. Carolene Products Co.*, 304 U.S. 144, 152 (1938).

22. James L. Oakes, " 'Property Rights' in Constitutional Analysis Today," *Washington Law Review* 56 (1981): 583, 608.

Chapter 8

1. *Lincoln Federal Labor Union v. Northwestern Iron & Metal Co.*, 335 U.S. 525, 536 (1949).

2. *Williamson v. Lee Optical Co.*, 348 U.S. 483, 487–88 (1955).

3. *Ferguson v. Skrupa*, 372 U.S. 726, 730 (1963).

4. Learned Hand, *The Bill of Rights* (Cambridge, Mass.: Harvard University Press, 1958), pp. 50–51.

5. *Lynch v. Household Finance Corp.*, 405 U.S. 538, 552 (1972).

6. For the law and economics perspective, see Frank H. Easterbrook, "Foreward: The Court and the Economic System," *Harvard Law Review* 98 (1984): 4.

7. Richard A. Epstein, "The Mistakes of 1937," *George Mason University Law Review* 11 (1988): 5, 20.

8. *United States Trust Co. v. New Jersey*, 431 U.S. 1, 16, 25 (1977).

9. Ibid., p. 33.

10. *Allied Structural Steel Co. v. Spannaus*, 438 U.S. 234, 241–42 (1978).

11. Ibid., p. 260.

12. *Keystone Bituminous Coal Association v. DeBenedictis*, 480 U.S. 470, 502 (1987).

13. *Armstrong v. United States*, 364 U.S. 40, 49 (1960).

14. *Berman v. Parker*, 348 U.S. 26, 33 (1954).

15. *Hawaii Housing Authority v. Midkiff*, 467 U.S. 229, 241 (1984).

16. *Agins v. City of Tiburon*, 447 U.S. 255, 260 (1980).

17. *Nollan v. California Coastal Commission,* 483 U.S. 825, 841 (1987).

18. Executive Order No. 12630, March 15, 1988, 53 FR 8859.

19. *Duquesne Light Co. v. Barasch,* 109 Sup. Ct. 609, 615 (1989).

20. *Allegheny Pittsburgh Coal Co. v. Webster County,* 488 U.S. 336, 343 (1989).

21. *Goldberg v. Kelly,* 397 U.S. 254, 265 (1970).

Chapter 9

1. Alexis de Tocqueville, *Democracy in America,* ed. J. Mayer, 13th ed. (originally published 1850) (New York: Harper & Row, 1966), pp. 638–39.

2. Herbert McClosky and John Zaller, *The American Ethos: Public Attitudes Toward Capitalism and Democracy* (Cambridge, Mass.: Harvard University Press, 1984), p. 140.

3. Alex Kozinski, "Forward: The Judiciary and the Constitution," in James A. Dorn and Henry G. Manne, eds., *Economic Liberties and the Judiciary* (Fairfax, Va.: George Mason University Press, 1987), p. xvii.

4. For an insightful discussion of Chief Justice Rehnquist's attitude toward property rights, see Sue Davis, *Justice Rehnquist and the Constitution* (Princeton, N.J.: Princeton University Press, 1989), pp. 97–131.

5. See William W. Van Alstyne, "The Recrudescence of Property Rights as the Foremost Principle of Civil Liberties: The First Decade of the Burger Court," *Law and Contemporary Problems* 43 (Summer 1980): 66–82.

Bibliographical Essay

In this bibliographical essay I acknowledge those scholars whose work was particularly valuable in writing this volume. The essay is selective and makes no attempt to include all of the literature dealing with property rights and constitutional law. Those seeking an extensive bibliography should consult the five-volume survey compiled by Kermit L. Hall, *A Comprehensive Bibliography of American Constitutional and Legal History* (1984). Readers may also turn to the excellent bibliographies contained in the leading treatises on constitutional history, those by Alfred H. Kelly, Winfred A. Harbison, and Herman Belz, *The American Constitution: Its Origins and Development* (7th ed., 1991); and Melvin I. Urofsky, *A March of Liberty: A Constitutional History of the United States* (1988).

General Works

There is no single book that systematically examines the constitutional protection of property rights throughout American history. Several prominent scholars, however, have written wide-ranging studies of constitutional history that give some attention to economic rights. Alfred H. Kelly, Winfred A. Harbison, and Herman Belz in *The American Constitution: Its Origins and Development*, have long dominated the field of constitutional history. Melvin I. Urofsky, *A March of Liberty: A Constitutional History of the United States,* offers a liberal interpretation of constitutional developments. Also helpful are William M. Wiecek, *Liberty Under Law: The Supreme Court in American Life* (1988); and Forrest McDonald, *A Constitutional History of the United States* (1982). Although somewhat dated, Charles Warren's classic *The Supreme Court in United States History* (rev. ed. 1926) remains an important source.

Numerous studies examine specific periods of constitutional history or Supreme Court activity. Readers will wish to begin with Kermit L. Hall, James W. Ely, Jr., Joel Grossman, and William M. Wiecek, eds., *The Oxford Companion to the Supreme Court of the United States* (1992), which includes numerous essays dealing with the Supreme Court and economic liberty. Harold M. Hyman and William M. Wiecek, *Equal Justice Under Law: Constitutional Development, 1835–1875* (1982), provides a fine treatment of property rights in the mid-nineteenth century. Another important work is John W. Semonche, *Charting the Future: The Supreme Court Responds to a Changing Society, 1890–1920* (1978). Loren P. Beth, *The Development of the American Constitution, 1877–1917* (1971), contains a judicious treatment of economic issues and pays welcome attention to state constitutional developments. Other helpful volumes include David P. Currie, *The Constitution in the Supreme Court: The First Hundred Years, 1789–1888* (1985); and Paul L. Murphy, *The Constitution in Crisis Times, 1918–1969* (1972).

Traditionally, constitutional and private law have been viewed as distinct topics. However, in his path-breaking book, *The Magic Mirror: Law in American History* (1989), Kermit L. Hall skillfully synthesizes constitutional and private law. Hall offers a sustained analysis of the judicial review of economic regulations. Lawrence M. Friedman's *A History of American Law* (2nd ed. 1985) focuses primarily on the growth of private law but also addresses some issues relating to property rights.

Relatively little scholarship has been specifically devoted to the place of property rights in constitutional history. But a good general study of American thinking about property is William B. Scott, *In Pursuit of Happiness: American Conceptions of Property from the Seventeenth to the Twentieth Century* (1977). It can be usefully complemented by reading Richard Schatter, *Private Property: The History of an Idea* (1951); and Harry N. Scheiber, "Economic Liberty and the Constitution" in *Essays in the History of Liberty: Seaver Institute Lectures at the Huntington Library* (1988).

Chapter 1: The Colonial Era

Constitutional historians have not given sustained attention to property rights during the colonial period. There are, however, a number of works that touch on the subject. A. E. Dick Howard's *The Road from Runnymede: Magna Carta and Constitutionalism in America* (1968), stresses the importance of Magna Carta and English common law. Elizabeth V. Mensch, "The Colonial Origins of Liberal Property Rights," *Buffalo Law Review* 31 (1982), examines conflicting notions of property ownership in colonial America.

Two general accounts of the colonial era treat land distribution practices and economic activity. See Clarence L. Ver Steeg, *The Formative Years, 1607–1763* (1964); and Wesley Frank Craven, *The Colonies in Transition, 1660–1713* (1968). In *America at 1750: A Social Portrait* (1971), Richard Hofstadter pictures colonial society in the mid-eighteenth century as largely middle class in nature. For early land use regulations, readers should see Carl Bridenbaugh, *Cities in the Wilderness: The First Century of Urban Life in America, 1625–1742* (1955), and *Cities in Revolt: Urban Life in America,* 1743–1776 (1955).

There are fine monographs on certain aspects of property ownership in colonial society. Landownership practices are ably covered by Marshall Harris in *Origin of the Land Tenure System* (1953). David S. Lovejoy, *The Glorious Revolution in America* (1972), examines the controversy over land titles and taxation policy under the Dominion of New England. The legal problems caused by New York's unique land system are explored by Patricia U. Bonomi, *A Factious People: Politics and Society in Colonial New York* (1971). The law of slavery is ably treated in William W. Wiecek, "The Statutory Law of Slavery and Race in the Thirteen Mainland Colonies of British America," *William and Mary Quarterly* 34 (1977).

Some authors have treated colonial economic development, but business and land regulations require more systematic attention from historians. Jon C. Teaford, *The Municipal Revolution in America: Origins of Modern Urban Government, 1650–1825* (1975), examines the municipal regulation of commercial activity. Henry W. Farnam's *Chapters in the History of Social Legislation in the United States to 1860* (1938) contains a wealth of information about land tenures, labor policy, trade regulations, public markets, and the assize of bread. Other valuable works include Shaw Livermore, *Early American Land Companies: Their Influence on Corporate Development* (1939); and Paton Yoder, "Tavern Regulation in Virginia: Rationale and Reality," *Virginia Magazine of History and Biography* 87 (1979). Taking of private property by colonial governments is analyzed in William B. Stoebuck, "A General Theory of Eminent Domain," *Washington Law Review* 47 (1972).

Chapter 2: The Revolution

There is a vast literature on the American Revolution, and the relationship of property rights to revolutionary constitutionalism is examined in several major works. Perhaps the best treatment is John Phillip Reid's *Constitutional History of the American Revolution: The Authority of Rights* (1986). Reid demonstrates the importance of property rights in revolutionary thought. Similarly, Edmund S. Morgan, *The Challenge of the American Revolution* (1976), emphasizes the link between property rights and liberty. William W. Fisher, III, "Ideology, Religion, and the Constitutional Protection of Private Property: 1760–1860," *Emory Law Journal* 39 (1990), explores the influence of religion and ideology in fashioning constitutional doctrines to safeguard property ownership. On the other hand, Gordon S. Wood, *The Creation of the American Republic, 1776–1787* (1969), contends that republican constitutional theory subordinated property ownership to the common good. Jefferson's attitude toward property is discussed in Stanley N. Katz, "Thomas Jefferson and the Right to Property in Revolutionary America," *Journal of Law and Economics* 19 (1976).

Scholars have worked on particular subjects relating to constitutional protection of economic rights. The confiscation of Loyalist property is examined by Wallace Brown in *The Good Americans: The Loyalists in the American Revolution* (1969). Charles F. Hobson, "The Recovery of British Debts in the Federal Circuit Court of Virginia, 1790 to 1797," *Virginia Magazine of History and Biography* 92 (1984), assesses the legal tangle arising from the sequestration of debts owed to British merchants.

Significant aspects of constitutional development occurred at the state level. There is an excellent analysis of property rights in the formation of state constitutions in Willi Paul Adams, *The First American Constitutions: Republican Ideology and the Making of the State Constitutions in the Revolutionary Era* (1980). The definitive study of property qualifications for voting is by Chilton Williamson, *American Suffrage from Property to Democracy 1760–1860* (1960). Herbert A. Johnson notes the concern for the security of private property in postrevolutionary South Carolina in "The Palmetto and the Oak: Law and Constitution in Early South Carolina, 1670–1800," in Kermit L. Hall and James W. Ely, Jr., eds., *An Uncertain Tradition: Constitutionalism and the History of the South* (1989). James W. Ely, Jr., "American Independence and the Law: A Study of Post-Revolutionary South Carolina Legislation," *Vanderbilt Law Review* 26 (1973), considers the affirmative use of the law and eminent domain to encourage economic growth in the Palmetto State.

Chapter 3: The New Constitutional Order

Historians have written extensively about framing the Constitution and the Bill of Rights. Several of these works give considerable attention to property rights in the constitution-drafting process. Forrest McDonald's superb *Novus Ordo Seclorum: The Intellectual Origins of the Constitution* (1985) analyzes the constitutional principles of the framers and examines as well the notion of private ownership in the eighteenth century. See also Forrest McDonald and Ellen Shapiro McDonald, *Requiem: Variations on Eighteenth-Century Themes* (1988), stressing the connection between the Constitution and the emergence of a free-market economy. For a valuable collection of essays discussing the importance of property rights in the formation of the Constitution, see Ellen Frankel Paul and Howard Dickman, eds., *Liberty, Property, and the Foundations of the American Constitution* (1989). Also useful is Stuart Bruchey, "The Impact of Concern for the Security of Property Rights on the Legal System of the Early American Republic," *Wisconsin Law Review* (1980).

The relationship between slavery and constitution making has been considered by numerous scholars. Among the more helpful are William M. Wiecek, *The Sources of Antislavery Constitutionalism in America, 1760–1848* (1977); and Paul Finkelman, "Slavery and the Constitutional Convention: Making a Covenant with Death," in Richard Beeman,

Stephen Botein, and Edward C. Carter, II, eds., *Beyond Confederation: Origins of the Constitution and American National Identity* (1987).

Charles A. Beard's controversial *An Economic Interpretation of the Constitution of the United States* (1913) contended that the framers sought to safeguard class interests by establishing a strong central government. Beard's views have been sharply criticized. For example, see Forrest McDonald, *E Pluribus Unum: The Formation of the American Republic, 1776–1790* (1965). The best study of the ratification struggle is by Jackson Turner Main, *The Antifederalists: Critics of the Constitution, 1781–1788* (1961). Jennifer Nedelsky's *Private Property and the Limits of American Constitutionalism: The Madisonian Framework and Its Legacy* (1990) stresses the central place of private property in the framers' conception of limited government, but appeared too late for full consideration in this volume.

The framing of the Bill of Rights has received surprisingly little treatment by scholars. Useful accounts of the development of the Bill of Rights are by Robert A. Rutland, *The Birth of the Bill of Rights, 1776–1791* (rev. ed. 1983); Irving Brant, *The Bill of Rights: Its Origin and Meaning* (1965); and Edward Dumbauld, *The Bill of Rights and What It Means Today* (1957). The background of the takings clause of the Fifth Amendment is explored by James W. Ely, Jr., " 'Property was certainly the principal object of society': The Fifth Amendment and the Origins of the Compensation Principle," unpublished manuscript.

Chapter 4: The Antebellum Era

Numerous works describe the development of judicial safeguards for property rights against legislative infringement before the Civil War. Edward S. Corwin, "The Basic Doctrine of American Constitutional Law," *Michigan Law Review* 12 (1914) and Lowell J. Howe, "The Meaning of 'Due Process of Law' Prior to the Adoption of the Fourteenth Amendment," *California Law Review* 18 (1918) remain valuable studies. The standard account of the contract clause is by Benjamin Fletcher Wright, *The Contract Clause of the Constitution* (1938). It can be usefully supplemented by Steven R. Boyd, "The Contract Clause and the Evolution of American Federalism, 1789–1815," *William and Mary Quarterly* 3rd ser. (1987). Felix Frankfurter's *The Commerce Clause*

Under Marshall, Taney and Waite (1937) traces interpretations of the commerce power.

A leading essay on eminent domain law is Harry N. Scheiber, ''The Road to *Munn:* Eminent Domain and the Concept of Public Purpose in the State Courts,'' in Donald Fleming and Bernard Bailyn, eds., *Law in American History* (1971). Scheiber points out that the state courts facilitated the reach of eminent domain authority by adopting broad notions of public purpose. Scheiber's essay can be profitably supplemented by Tony A. Freyer's ''Reassessing the Impact of Eminent Domain in Early American Economic Development,'' *Wisconsin Law Review* (1981).

Some of the best work on the constitutional protection of property can be found in biographies of prominent judges and attorneys. R. Kent Newmyer's outstanding *Supreme Court Justice Joseph Story: Statesman of the Old Republic* (1985) assesses Story's commitment to property and commerce. Robert K. Faulkner, *The Jurisprudence of John Marshall* (1968), emphasizes Marshall's devotion to property rights as a means of encouraging economic production. For biographies of important state court judges, see Leonard W. Levy, *The Law of the Commonwealth and Chief Justice Shaw* (1957), and John T. Horton, *James Kent: A Study in Conservatism, 1763–1847* (1939). Maurice G. Baxter's *Daniel Webster & the Supreme Court* (1966) sketches Webster's high regard for economic rights.

There are some useful studies of particular decisions dealing with property and commerce. Particularly rewarding are those by C. Peter Magrath, *Yazoo, Law and Politics in the New Republic; The Case of Fletcher v. Peck* (1966); Stanley I. Kutler, *Privilege and Creative Destruction: The Charles River Bridge Case* (1971); Maurice G. Baxter, *The Steamboat Monopoly; Gibbons v. Ogden, 1824* (1972); and Elizabeth B. Monroe, ''Spanning the Commerce Clause: The Wheeling Bridge Case, 1850–1856,'' *American Journal of Legal History* 32 (1988).

Chapter 5: The Gilded Age

The constitutional history of the Civil War has important implications for property rights. Both Harold M. Hyman, *A More Perfect Union: The*

Impact of the Civil War and Reconstruction on the Constitution (1973);
and James G. Randall, *Constitutional Problems Under Lincoln* (rev. ed.
1951) offer cogent analyses of the emancipation of slaves as well as the
confiscation of Confederate property.

Scholars have hotly debated the emergence of laissez-faire constitutionalism and economic due process during the late nineteenth century.
The best account of the laissez-faire philosophy is Michael Les Benedict's "Laissez-Faire and Liberty: A Re-Evaluation of the Meaning and
Origins of Laissez-Faire Constitutionalism," *Law and History Review* 3
(1985), which shows that conservative judges and scholars were genuinely interested in liberty. Other valuable studies from the same perspective are Charles W. McCurdy, "Justice Field and the Jurisprudence of
Government–Business Relations: Some Parameters of Laissez-Faire
Constitutionalism, 1863–1897," *Journal of American History* 61
(1975), and Robert E. Garner, "Justice Brewer and Substantive Due
Process: A Conservative Court Revisited," *Vanderbilt Law Review* 18
(1965). Herbert Hovenkamp, "The Political Economy of Substantive
Due Process," *Stanford Law Review* 40 (1988), concludes that the
formulation of economic due process was guided by the prevailing
economic ideology. In contrast, Arnold M. Paul, *Conservative Crisis
and the Rule of Law: Attitudes of Bar and Bench, 1887–1895* (1960),
seeks to explain laissez-faire constitutionalism as a response to perceived
threats to the social order. Edward S. Corwin, "The Supreme Court and
the Fourteenth Amendment," *Michigan Law Review* 7 (1909), provides
an early but still useful look at the growth of economic due process.

A number of fine works have studied the leading scholarly proponents
of laissez-faire constitutionalism. See, for example, Alan Jones,
"Thomas Cooley and 'Laissez-Faire Constitutionalism': A Reconsideration," *Journal of American History* 53 (1967); and David N. Mayer,
"The Jurisprudence of Christopher G. Tiedeman: A Study in the Failure
of Laissez-Faire Constitutionalism," *Missouri Law Review* 93 (1990).
Benjamin R. Twiss, *Lawyers and the Constitution: How Laissez-Faire
Came to the Supreme Court* (1942), examines the role of prominent
lawyers who advocated laissez-faire before the courts.

Scholars have shown renewed interest in railroad and utility rate
regulations. Mary Cornelia Porter, "That Commerce Shall Be Free: A
New Look at the Old Laissez-Faire Court," *Supreme Court Review 1976*

(1977), demonstrates that the judicial review of rates was designed to encourage investment capital by guaranteeing a fair return. Stephen A. Siegel, "Understanding the *Lochner* Era: Lessons from the Controversy over Railroad and Utility Rate Regulation," *Virginia Law Review* 70 (1984), considers the substantive criteria employed in judicial review of rate regulations. Also useful are Charles Fairman, "The So-called Granger Cases, Lord Hale, and Justice Bradley," *Stanford Law Review* 5 (1953); Herbert Hovenkamp, "Regulatory Conflict in the Gilded Age: Federalism and the Railroad Problem," *Yale Law Journal* 97 (1988), and James W. Ely, Jr., "The Railroad Question Revisited: *Chicago, Milwaukee and St. Paul Railway* and Constitutional Limits on State Regulations," unpublished manuscript. For a discussion of the movement toward judicial scrutiny of rate regulations in an important state see Katha G. Hartley, "*Spring Valley Water Works v. San Francisco:* Defining Economic Rights in San Francisco," *Western Legal History* 3 (1990).

A general examination of judicial protection of property rights during the Gilded Age is David P. Currie, "The Constitution in the Supreme Court: The Protection of Economic Interests, 1889–1910," *University of Chicago Law Review* 52 (1985). Specific controversies have been the focus of more specialized inquiry. For the legal tender litigation, see Kenneth W. Dam, "The Legal Tender Cases," *Supreme Court Review 1981* (1982). The question of state and municipal debt repudiation is ably explored by John V. Orth, *The Judicial Power of the United States: The Eleventh Amendment in the Constitution* (1987). Although in need of revision, Charles Warren's *Bankruptcy in United States History* (1935) remains the classic account of early bankruptcy laws.

Important insights into judicial thinking about property rights are provided in biographies of important justices. Worthwhile studies include those by Charles Fairman, *Mr. Justice Miller and the Supreme Court, 1862–1890* (1939); Willard L. King, *Melville Weston Fuller: Chief Justice of the United States, 1888–1910* (1950); Carol Brent Swisher, *Stephen Field: Craftsman of the Law* (1930); and C. Peter Magrath, *Morrison R. Waite: The Triumph of Character* (1963). Robert G. McClosky, *American Conservation in the Age of Enterprise, 1865–1910* (1951) investigates judicial acceptance of economic due process.

Chapter 6: Progressivism and Conservatism

Property rights in twentieth-century constitutional history warrant greater exploration. Aside from studies of particular issues scholars have given only limited attention to the constitutional protection of economic liberty.

The fine collection of essays by Ellen Frankel Paul and Howard Dickman, eds., *Liberty, Property, and Government: Constitutional Interpretation Before the New Deal* (1989), offers a good introduction to pre–New Deal developments. An important article by Melvin I. Urofsky, "State Courts and Protective Legislation During the Progressive Era: A Reevaluation," *Journal of American History* 72 (1985), contends that judges ultimately sustained most of the protective laws. Herbert Hovenkamp, "The First Great Law & Economics Movement," *Stanford Law Review* 42 (1990), traces changes in economic thought during the Progressive era.

Several works assess the judicial handling of social and economic legislation. Paul Kens, *Judicial Power and Reform Politics: The Anatomy of Lochner v. New York* (1990), is a rewarding account of a famous decision. See also Frank R. Strong, "The Economic Philosophy of Lochner: Emergence, Embrasure and Emasculation," *Arizona Law Review* 15 (1973). Stephen B. Wood, *Constitutional Politics in the Progressive Era: Child Labor and the Law* (1968), illuminates the drive to eliminate child labor. Aviam Soifer, "The Paradox of Paternalism and Laissez-Faire Constitutionalism: United States Supreme Court, 1888–1921," *Law and History Review* 5 (1987), contends that the justices sought to contain paternalism and defend economic individualism.

Land use regulation and eminent domain have received only scant attention. Lawrence M. Friedman, "A Search for Seizure: Pennsylvania Coal Co. v. Mahon in Context," *Law and History Review* 4 (1986), offers a cogent analysis of the landmark case that established the doctrine of a regulatory taking. Judicial reliance on property rights to strike down residential segregation statutes is described in Roger L. Rice, "Residential Segregation by Law, 1910–1917," *Journal of Southern History* 34 (1968); and Richard A. Epstein, "Race and the Police Power: 1890 to 1937," *Washington and Lee Law Review* 46 (1989). For a helpful study of the adoption of the Sixteenth Amendment, see David E. Kyvig, "Can the Constitution Be Amended? The Battle over the Income Tax, 1895–1913," *Prologue* 20 (1988).

Biographies of prominent conservative justices cast light on their property-conscious philosophy. See Joel Francis Paschal, *Mr. Justice Sutherland: A Man Against the State* (1951); and Alpheus T. Mason, *William Howard Taft: Chief Justice* (1965). For the judicial career of leading Progressives, readers should consult Melvin I. Urofsky, *Louis D. Brandeis and the Progressive Tradition* (1981); and G. Edward White, *The American Judicial Tradition: Profiles of Leading American Judges* (1976).

Chapter 7: The New Deal

Historians have long been interested in the constitutional changes introduced by the New Deal. Scholars, however, have focused more on the political dimensions of the clash between the Supreme Court and the New Deal than on the constitutional protection of economic interests. The initial opposition of the Supreme Court to much of the New Deal program is well covered by William E. Leuchtenburg, *Franklin D. Roosevelt and the New Deal, 1932–1940* (1963). Robert G. McClosky, "Economic Due Process and the Supreme Court: An Exhumation and Reburial," *Supreme Court Review 1962* (1963), pictures the Court's retreat from defending property as dictated by political realities. See also Note, "The New Deal Court: Emergence of a New Reason," *Columbia Law Review* 90 (1990). Richard A. Epstein's "The Mistakes of 1937," *George Mason University Law Review* 11 (1988), is a sharp criticism of New Deal constitutionalism for downplaying economic rights and extending federal power over the economy.

A number of works have explored leading decisions or aspects of New Deal policy. Geoffrey P. Miller, "The True Story of Carolene Products," *Supreme Court Review 1987* (1988), is a valuable analysis of the subordination of property rights by New Deal constitutionalism. The impact of constitutional change with respect to the scope of the commerce power is treated in Richard C. Cortner, *The Wagner Act Cases* (1964). For a vigorous critique of the New Deal's expansive interpretation of the commerce clause, see Richard A. Epstein, "The Proper Scope of the Commerce Power," *Virginia Law Review* 73 (1987). Carolyn C. Jones, "Class Tax to Mass Tax: The Role of Propaganda in the Expansion of the Income Tax During World War II," *Buffalo Law Review* 37 (1989), explores New Deal income tax policy.

One of the best ways to understand the diminished constitutional protection for economic interests is through the study of judges and attorneys. Among the most rewarding judicial biographies are those by Charles A. Leonard, *A Search for a Judicial Philosophy: Mr. Justice Roberts and the Constitutional Revolution of 1937* (1971); Alpheus T. Mason, *Harlan Fiske Stone: Pillar of the Law* (1956); and C. Herman Pritchett, *The Roosevelt Court: A Study in Judicial Politics and Values, 1937–1947* (1948). For the role of attorneys in shaping liberal legal culture, see Peter H. Irons, *The New Deal Lawyers* (1982). The perspective of a leading conservative spokesman is examined in William H. Harbaugh's excellent *Lawyer's Lawyer: The Life of John W. Davis* (1973).

Chapter 8: The Regulatory State

For many years following World War II, the question of economic rights was of little interest to either judges or scholars. Learned Hand's *The Bill of Rights* (1958) questioned the dichotomy between property and personal rights, but most observers gave little heed.

In the 1980s the scholarly debate over the constitutional protection of property was reopened for the first time since the New Deal. Thoughtful observations about the constitutional significance of economic liberty may be found in William W. Van Alstyne, "The Recrudescence of Property Rights as the Foremost Principle of Civil Liberties: The First Decade of the Burger Court," *Law and Contemporary Problems* 43 (1980); and James L. Oakes, "'Property Rights' in Constitutional Analysis Today," *Washington Law Review* 56 (1981). Sue Davis, *Justice Rehnquist and the Constitution* (1989), provides a cogent analysis of Chief Justice William Rehnquist's views on property rights.

A group of conservative scholars has sparked a lively discourse by urging reinvigorated constitutional protection of economic interests. Bernard H. Siegan, *Economic Liberties and the Constitution* (1980), provides a good overview. Richard A. Epstein has written extensively about the constitutional provisions that bear on property rights. See his *Takings: Private Property and the Power of Eminent Domain* (1985), and "Toward a Revitalization of the Contract Clause," *University of Chicago Law Review* 51 (1984). Stephen Macedo, *The New Right v. The*

Constitution (1986), also criticizes the Supreme Court's neglect of economic liberties. Other useful works include those by James A. Dorn and Henry G. Manne, eds., *Economic Liberties and the Judiciary* (1987); Clint Bolick, *Unfinished Business: A Civil Rights Strategy for America's Third Century* (1990); and Note, "Resurrecting Economic Rights: The Doctrine of Economic Due Process Reconsidered," *Harvard Law Review* 103 (1990).

Other scholars have challenged this renewed interest in property rights. See Bernard Schwartz, *The New Right and the Constitution: Turning Back the Legal Clock* (1990); Thomas C. Grey, "The Malthusian Constitution," *University of Miami Law Review* 41 (1986); and Herman Schwartz, "Property Rights and the Constitution: Will the Ugly Duckling Become a Swan?" *American University Law Review* 37 (1987). Cass R. Sunstein's *After the Rights Revolution: Reconceiving the Regulatory State* (1990) defends economic regulation against attacks based on free-market principles.

Supreme Court decisions dealing with land use regulations and the takings clause have generated a large law review commentary. For a particularly thoughtful assessment, see Carol M. Rose, "Property Rights, Regulatory Regimes and the New Takings Jurisprudence—An Evolutionary Approach," *Tennessee Law Review* 57 (1990).

The scope of the commerce power is treated in Paul R. Benson, Jr., *The Supreme Court and the Commerce Clause, 1937–1970* (1970). Mark V. Tushnet, "Rethinking the Dormant Commerce Clause," *Wisconsin Law Review* (1979), ably scrutinizes the dormant commerce power. Richard C. Cortner illuminates an important decision in *The Arizona Train Limit Case: Southern Pacific Co. v. Arizona* (1970).

The concept of "new property" is explored by Charles A. Reich, in "The New Property," *Yale Law Journal* 73 (1964). Martin Shapiro's "The Supreme Court's 'Return' to Economic Regulation," *Studies in American Political Development* 1 (1986), questions the conventional view that the Court abandoned economic rights after 1937 and notes the vitality of economic due process in the development of "new property" and in the interpretation of regulatory legislation.

Index of Cases

Index